TOWER HAMLETS PUBLIC LIBRARY

910 000 00225597

Microsoft

# Office 2007

**idea**

Library Learning Information

To renew this item call:

**020 7364 4332**

or visit

**www.ideastore.co.uk**

TOWER HAMLETS

Created and managed by Tower Hamlets Council

WITHDRAWN

PEARSON

Prentice
Hall

Harlow, England • London • New York • Boston • San Franc... • Toronto • Sydney • Singapore • Hong Kong
Tokyo • Seoul • Taipei • New Delhi • Cape Town • Madrid • Mexico City • Amsterdam • Munich • Paris • Milan

**PEARSON EDUCATION LIMITED**

Edinburgh Gate
Harlow CM20 2JE
Tel: +44 (0)1279 623623
Fax: +44 (0)1279 431059
Website: www.pearsoned.co.uk

| LONDON BOROUGH TOWER HAMLETS | |
|---|---|
| 910 000 00225597 | |
| HJ | 23-Jul-2010 |
| 005.5 | £10.99 |
| THISWH | |

First published in Great Britain in 2009

© Greg Holden 2009

The right of Greg Holden to be identified as author of this work has been asserted
by him in accordance with the Copyright, Designs and Patents Act 1988.

ISBN: 978–0–273–72355–4

British Library Cataloguing-in-Publication Data
A catalogue record for this book is available from the British Library.

Library of Congress Cataloging-in-Publication Data
A catalog record for this book is available from the Library of Congress.

All rights reserved. No part of this publication may be reproduced, stored in a retrieval
system, or transmitted in any form or by any means, electronic, mechanical, photocopying,
recording or otherwise, without either the prior written permission of the publisher
or a licence permitting restricted copying in the United Kingdom issued by the
Copyright Licensing Agency Ltd, Saffron House, 6–10 Kirby Street, London EC1N 8TS.
This book may not be lent, resold, hired out or otherwise disposed of by way of trade in
any form of binding or cover other than that in which it is published, without the prior
consent of the Publishers.

Microsoft screen shots reprinted with permission from Microsoft Corporation.

10 9 8 7 6 5 4 3 2
13 12 11 10 09

Designed by pentacorbig, High Wycombe

Typeset in 11/14 pt ITC Stone Sans by 30
Printed by Ashford Colour Press Ltd., Gosport

The publisher's policy is to use paper manufactured from sustainable forests.

Microsoft
# Office
# 2007

in Simple
steps

Greg Holden

# Use your computer with confidence

Get to grips with practical computing tasks with minimal time, fuss and bother.

*In Simple Steps guides* guarantee immediate results. They tell you everything you need to know on a specific application; from the most essential tasks to master, to every activity you'll want to accomplish, through to solving the most common problems you'll encounter.

## Helpful features

To build your confidence and help you to get the most out of your computer, practical hints, tips and shortcuts feature on every page:

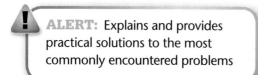 **ALERT:** Explains and provides practical solutions to the most commonly encountered problems

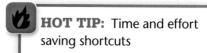 **HOT TIP:** Time and effort saving shortcuts

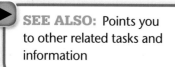 **SEE ALSO:** Points you to other related tasks and information

 **DID YOU KNOW?** Additional features to explore

**WHAT DOES THIS MEAN?**

Jargon and technical terms explained in plain English

## Practical. Simple. Fast.

in Simple steps

## Dedication:

Once again to Polina

# Contents at a glance

## 9 Getting organised with Outlook

Top 10 Office 2007 Problems Solved

# Contents

## 2 Working with text

## 3 Working with art and photos

## 4 Applying themes and formatting

## 5 Creating a Word document

## 6 Working with Excel spreadsheets

# 7 Assembling PowerPoint presentations

# 8 Creating an Access database

## 9 Getting organised with Outlook

## Top 10 Office 2007 Problems Solved

# Top 10 Office 2007 Tips

# Tip 1: Launch an Office application

If you've used Windows before, you probably know that the place to start any application is the Start button on the taskbar. By default, the Start button is in the lower left-hand corner of your desktop, though you can drag the taskbar to other sides if you wish. Vista gives you several options for finding Office applications among your installed programs.

Do one of the following:

**1** Type the name of the application you want (for example, Outlook) in the box next to the Start button.

**2** Click All Programs.

**3** If you typed the name, double-click it when it appears in the Start menu.

**4** Single-click Microsoft Office, then choose the application you want from the list.

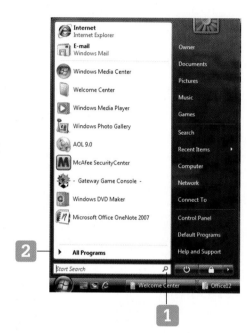

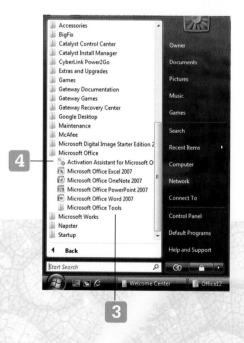

**HOT TIP:** If you used an application recently, click the Start button. The application's name will appear in the Start menu.

**? DID YOU KNOW?**

You can start any Office application by creating a desktop shortcut for it or by 'pinning' it to the Start menu. Right-click the application's icon (in Program Files\Microsoft Office\Office12) and choose Pin to Start Menu or Shortcut from the context menu.

# Tip 2: Select and edit text

Once you have learned to select the text you want (see Chapter 2), you can edit the text so it looks and reads the way that you want. Most of the time, that means you'll want to cut, copy or paste text from one location to another. You can use keyboard commands for any of those functions, but you can also use a mouse to drag and drop, copy or move text from one file to another or from one location to another in the same file.

**1** Use one of the techniques described in Chapter 2, or click at the beginning of the text you want to arrange, then hold the mouse button down and drag over the text. The text is highlighted to indicate that it has been selected.

**2** Then do one of the following:

- Type your new text to immediately replace the highlighted text
- Press Backspace or Delete (Del) to delete the text and then type the new text.

**1**

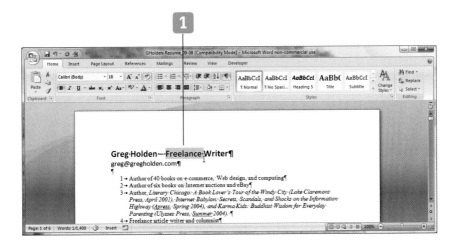

**?** **DID YOU KNOW?**
You can double-click a word to select it or triple-click a paragraph to select it.

# Tip 3: Insert an image

Whether you have chosen an image from Office's Clip Art libraries or a photo taken with your digital camera, you can easily add the image to a document. You can add a file from a CD-ROM, directly from your digital camera, from a flash, USB, drive or from a file on your hard disk. Before you add an image, you can view a thumbnail to make sure that it's the one you want.

**1** Click the Insert tab.

**2** Click Picture.

**3** Click one of your Favorite links or the dropdown list arrow to locate an image.

**4** Click an image file.

**5** Click Insert.

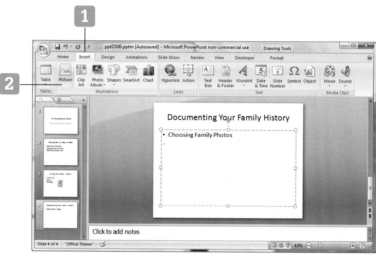

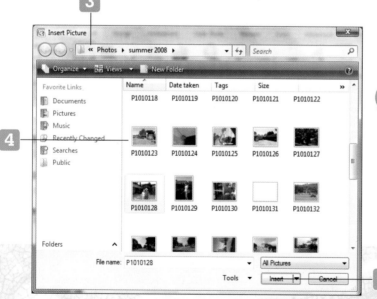

**?** **DID YOU KNOW?**
You can link to a file as well as insert it by clicking the dropdown list arrow next to Insert and choosing **Link to File**.

# Tip 4: Apply a theme

Office makes two kinds of design themes available to you: predesigned themes that come ready to use and customised themes that you can create yourself. Each theme contains a palette of 12 complementary colours as well as preselected fonts and other special effects. You don't see the colours all at once – some are accent colours, used for elements such as drop shadows or hyperlinks. You can view and change any of the colours if you want to match certain colours that you use in your other publications.

**1** Open the file to which you want to apply a theme.

**2** Click either the Page Layout or Design tab.

**3** Click the All Themes button to display the gallery of available themes.

**4** Click the theme you want (or Browse for Themes for more options) and that theme's fonts and colours will be applied to the current document.

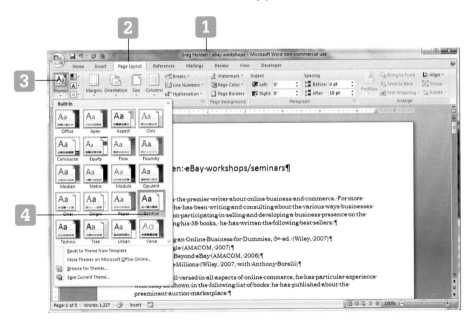

**! ALERT:** If you are using Word, your document must be saved in Word 2007 format rather than as a Word 97-2003 (Compatibility Mode) document in order to use themes.

**? DID YOU KNOW?** When you pass your mouse arrow over a theme, the colours appear in a live preview in the document that is currently open.

# Tip 5: Create an outline

An outline is a hierarchical way of organising a set of information into categories and subcategories. You can either create an outline from scratch while in Outline view, or else convert the items in a bulleted or numbered list into an outline. The steps given below will get you started if you want to create an outline from scratch.

1 Open a new file and click the Page Layout tab.

2 Click the Outline View button.

3 Type a heading for your outline, then press Enter.

4 If you need to change the heading level to a higher or lower one, position the insertion point at the beginning of the heading and click the Promote or Demote buttons.

5 Move to the next line and type a subheading or item in the outline. As before, click the Promote or Demote buttons to change the level as needed.

6 When you've finished, click Close Outline View.

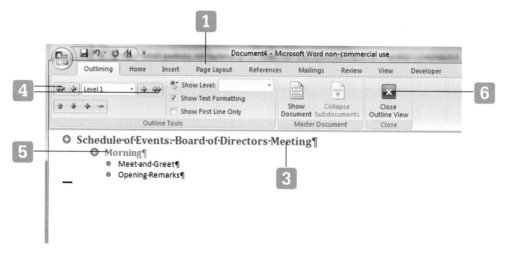

**? DID YOU KNOW?**

You can also position the cursor anywhere in a heading and click the Move Up or Move Down buttons until it is positioned correctly in the outline.

# Tip 6: Enter values in an Excel worksheet

Entering values in worksheet cells is one of the basic tasks associated with spreadsheets. Values can take the form of whole numbers, decimals, percentages or dates. You can enter numeric values by either using the number keys at the top of your keyboard or pressing the Num Lock key.

**1** Click the cell where you want to enter a value.

**2** Type the value.

**3** Press Enter.

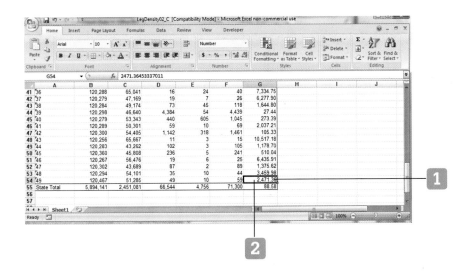

**HOT TIP:** Rather than pressing the Enter key, you can click the Enter button on the Formula bar.

**? DID YOU KNOW?**

When you begin to enter a date or time, Excel recognises the entries (if they correspond to one of its built-in date or time formats) and changes the information to fit its default date or time format.

# Tip 7: Insert a PowerPoint template

If you don't want to create a presentation from scratch, turn to the templates that Office 2007 provides for you. PowerPoint comes with a selection of pre-installed templates. If you don't find the one you want, you'll find a wide selection on Microsoft Office Online. You can choose templates for everything from invitations to agendas. By starting with a template, you get a suggested set of slides that you can modify to fit your own needs.

**1** Click the Office button.

**2** Click New.

**3** Click Installed Templates to view the templates that come with PowerPoint.

**4** Click one of the categories under Microsoft Office Online to view templates online.

**5** Select the template you want.

**6** Click Create.

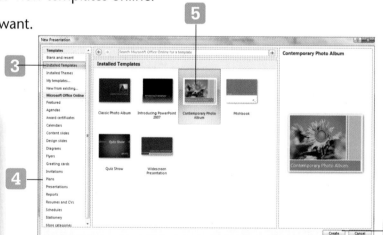

**? DID YOU KNOW?**

To download the Microsoft Office Online templates, you need to use Internet Explorer rather than another browser. An Active X control may have to be installed so that you can view and install the template you want.

**! ALERT:** Some of the templates at Microsoft Office Online were submitted by individuals rather than by Microsoft itself. Make sure that there aren't any permissions issues before you copy a template.

# Tip 8: Manage Access database objects

The objects that make up a database are there to help you track and work with your data, but you don't have to stick with the default names for objects. You can create new objects, hide some objects or delete them. That way, each database will have only the selection of objects that you need.

**1** Double-click an object in the Navigation pane to open it or right-click the object to change its design.

**2** Choose Delete from the context menu to delete the object.

**3** Click the Create tab.

**4** Click the button for the type of object you want to create.

**5** Work with the object when it opens in the Reading pane.

**6** Click the object's Close button when you have finished.

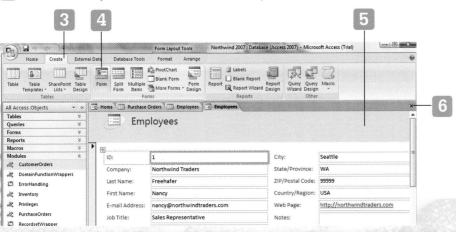

## DID YOU KNOW?

The AutoCorrect feature automatically renames objects. When you rename an object, any subsequent objects that use the object you have just renamed are given that name as well. Click the Office button, click Access Options, click Current Database, then select the Name AutoCorrect options you want.

# Tip 9: Add a new contact

Contacts are fundamental pieces of information that you can track and work with in Outlook. A 'contact' is a person or business you need to communicate with, by phone, fax, IM, text or email. Outlook can help you with all of these media: it gives you a way to store names, addresses and contact information, as well as other essential information about each contact, such as birthdays, account information, company names or titles.

**1** Click the Contacts view button in the Navigation pane.

**2** Click New in the toolbar.

**3** When the Contact window opens, fill in the contact information. The Contact window contains its own set of Ribbon tabs: Contact, Insert, Format Text and Developer.

**4** When you enter a phone number, fill in your current location in the Location Information dialogue box and then click OK.

**5** Click Details on the Contact tab in the Show group and fill in more detailed information about the contact.

**6** Click the Save & Close button to the left of the Contact tab in the Actions group.

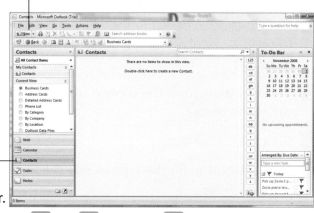

**HOT TIP:** Double-click anywhere in the Reading pane to create a new contact entry.

**? DID YOU KNOW?**

In the process of creating a contact, you also create an electronic business card, which you can share with others as an email attachment.

# Tip 10: Send an email message

When you have the text of your email message and attached files and signatures as needed, you can send it. You can send and receive messages at the same time, as well as control the way Outlook sends messages. When you send a message, Outlook moves it to the Outbox folder, where it stays while Outlook connects to your email server and sends the mail.

**1** Create your message.

**2** Click the Send button to simply send the message, or click the Send/Receive down arrow in the toolbar to choose a send option:

- Send All sends all messages that are ready to send in all email accounts
- Send <account name> sends only messages that are ready in the specified email account.

**3** Choose Send/Receive Settings at the bottom of the list, then choose Send/Receive Groups to change the way Outlook sends and receives email.

**4** Click the New, Edit, Copy, Remove, or Rename buttons to change the settings for the selected account group or all accounts.

**5** Click or untick the tickboxes for the send and receive options you want.

**6** Click Close, then click OK.

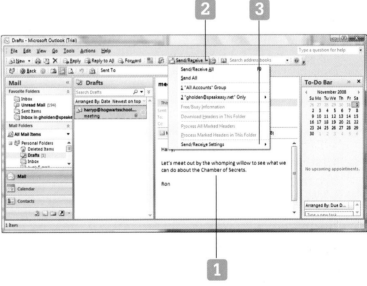

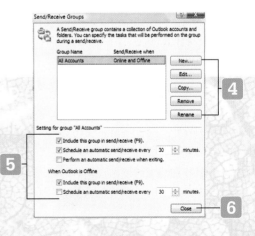

**? DID YOU KNOW?**
To insert a miniature version of your calendar in an email message, click the Insert tab at the top of the message window, then click the Calendar button.

# 1 Getting acquainted with Office 2007

# Introduction

Congratulations on choosing Microsoft® Office 2007 as your productivity and information management tool. You'll be happy to discover that Office 2007's suite of programs provides you with everything that you need to manage data, text and presentations and to communicate with anyone online. Each of the programs – Access, Word, Excel, PowerPoint, Outlook and Publisher – is designed to perform specialised tasks, but they are also closely integrated with one another and with the Web as well.

If you have used previous versions of Office, you'll find a few surprises. For instance, you'll notice right away that the File menu has gone and the top of the application window is more complex and feature-rich than ever before (it's called the Ribbon). Don't worry, though, none of your favourite menu commands or functions is missing – they've just been moved around so that you can find them more easily. Once you've acquainted yourself with the new interface and features, you'll find that Office 2007 is easier to use, faster and more reliable than previous versions.

If this is your first time using Office, you'll find each program's learning curve especially easy to climb. That's due in part to the suite's intuitive nature and in part to visual aids such as ToolTips, task panes, improved status bar and extensive Help options. You don't need to be a computer guru to use Office. In this first chapter you'll learn everything you need to know to get up and running with any of the Office 2007 applications.

*Important*: Office 2007 comes in several editions and computer manufacturers often add their own touches. As a result, your screen may not look exactly like what you'll see in the screenshots in this book, but it'll be close.

# Manually activate Office 2007

Normally, the process of activating Office is automatic. You enter your product key and the Activation Wizard starts up, prompting you to activate. You may choose to activate at a later time (for instance, if you're not currently connected to the Internet). If you ever want to manually activate the program, you can do so from the Office button in the upper left-hand corner of an Access, Excel, Word or PowerPoint window.

**1** Click the Office button.

**2** Click the Options button for the program you are using.

**3** Click Resources.

**4** Click Activate, and follow the steps in the Wizard.

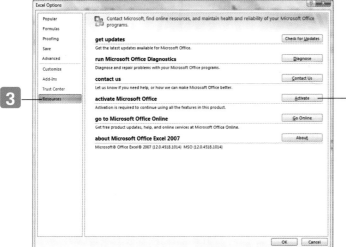

## DID YOU KNOW?

You can activate manually using InfoPath, Outlook, Publisher, Project or another Office 2007 application, but you need to click Help and then choose Activate Product. Then, follow the steps in the Activation Wizard.

# Launch an Office application

If you've used Windows before, you probably know that the place to start any application is the Start button on the taskbar. By default, the Start button is in the lower left-hand corner of your desktop, though you can drag the taskbar to other sides if you wish. Vista gives you several options for finding Office applications among your installed programs.

Do one of the following:

**1** Type the name of the application you want (for example, Outlook) in the box next to the Start button.

**2** Click All Programs.

**3** If you typed the name, double-click it when it appears in the Start menu.

**4** Single-click Microsoft Office, then choose the application you want from the list.

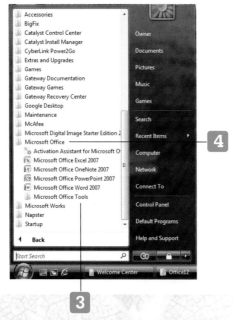

**HOT TIP:** If you used an application recently, click the Start button. The application's name will appear in the Start menu.

**? DID YOU KNOW?**

You can start any Office application by creating a desktop shortcut for it or by 'pinning' it to the Start menu. Right-click the application's icon (in Program Files\Microsoft Office\Office12) and choose Pin to Start Menu or Shortcut from the context menu.

**! ALERT:** Don't type 'Microsoft' as the program name – you'll end up with a long list of applications. Simply type 'Word' or 'Excel' and so on.

# Work with the Office program window

Once you open an Office application, the program window opens. The specifics vary from one program to another, but, if you learn some of the common features, you'll be able to use the program more easily. These include the Office button, the Quick Access Toolbar, the status bar, the Ribbon and Zoom controls. They are common to all of the Office applications and many are new to Office 2007. Some, like the main program window, will have to be discovered as you work with the application. You can click on many of the main features to learn what they do.

**1** Office Button: click the Office button. It replaces the File menu and performs many other functions as well.

**2** Quick Access Toolbar: click to perform common functions, such as save, undo and redo. Customise the toolbar to add more commands.

**3** Ribbon: click tools and choose commands grouped by category in different tabs.

**4** Program window: work with presentations, data, text or other content here.

**5** Zoom controls: all Office applications let you zoom in or out using a slider or buttons.

**6** View buttons: click to switch between views.

**7** Status bar: shows details about current document.

**? DID YOU KNOW?**
The small arrows in the bottom right corner of some tool groups in the Ribbon open dialogue boxes or task panes.

**▶ SEE ALSO:** See Open an existing Office file and Change preferences in this chapter for more of the many functions that the Office button can perform in addition to previous File menu functions.

# Open a new blank Office file

If you are launching an Office application, a new blank document opens automatically so that you can start working with it. If you already have the application open, you can open as many new presentation, spreadsheet, word processing, database or publication files as you wish. Each document is assigned a generic name, such as Book1 or Document1, so you need to save the file with a more specific name to be able to find it easily.

**1** Click the Office button.

**2** Click New.

**3** Make sure Blank and recent is selected in the Templates task pane on the left.

**4** Click Blank document.

**5** Click Create. A new blank file appears in the current Office application window.

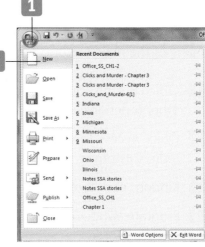

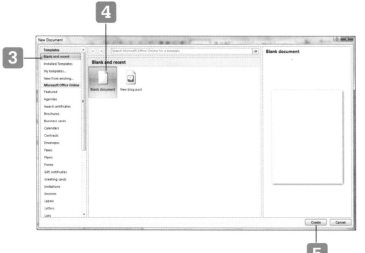

**HOT TIP:** You can save time by pressing Ctrl+N instead of clicking the Office button and choosing New. Pressing Ctrl+N causes a new blank file to appear instantly.

**WHAT DOES THIS MEAN?**

**Task pane** A miniature window that opens within the main Office program window.

**Template** A preconfigured document that serves as a shortcut so you don't have to create the file from scratch.

# Open an existing Office file

Most of the time, you will be opening files that you have already edited rather than creating new ones. As usual, Windows gives you several options, and each has its advantages. If you click the Office button, you can either choose Open to locate the file, or open the file from a list of recent documents. If you double-click the file's icon, you can launch the application as well if it's not open already.

**1** Click Office.

**2** Click Open.

**3** Choose an open from the Files of type list if you want to choose from files of a certain type.

**4** Click the file you want and then click Open or, if you want to control exactly how the file is opened, choose one of the available opens by clicking the down arrow next to Open:

- Open Read-Only opens the file so it can't be edited

- Open as Copy opens a copy of the file, not the original

- Open in Browser opens the Web file in a Web browser

- Open with Transform

- Open and Repair allows you to open a damaged file.

---

**HOT TIP:** You can also open a file and launch an Office application simultaneously if you double-click the file's icon in the Computer window, the Documents list or Windows Explorer.

**? DID YOU KNOW?**

If you have worked recently on the file that you want to open, chances are it will be listed with other recent files when you click the Office button. Click the file's name to open it.

# Explore the Ribbon

The Ribbon is probably the single most noticeable change in Office 2007 compared with previous versions. It replaces the system of menus and toolbars you're probably familiar with. The Ribbon is always located at the top of the Office window.

The Ribbon is divided into tabs and each tab contains multiple groups of tools. Each command button in a tool group performs a specific function.

1. Click each of the tabs in turn to display their contents. For instance, open Word and click the Insert tab.

2. Click Table to see the dropdown options beneath it.

3. Drag your mouse down and to the right to draw a table in the current program window.

4. To display a contextual tab (a tab that appears only when needed based on what you're doing), click SmartArt.

5. Click one of the SmartArt options.

6. Click OK.

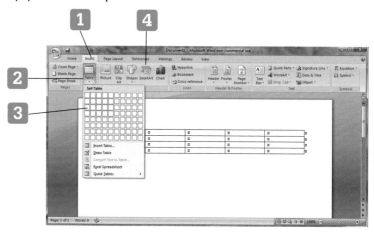

**? DID YOU KNOW?**

If you want to use keyboard shortcuts instead of Ribbon commands, press the Alt or F10 keys. KeyTips will appear over each feature in the current view. To hide the KeyTips, press the Alt or F10 key again.

7 Click one of the SmartArt objects you just added. The Design and Format contextual tabs appear.

8 Use the arrows to change how long to wait before the screensaver is enabled.

9 If desired, click On to resume and display logon screen which requires a password to log back onto the computer.

10 Click OK.

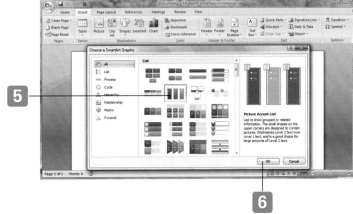

5

6

7

**HOT TIP:** If you need more screen space, you can minimise the Ribbon by double-clicking the tab that is currently in front. Alternatively, click the list arrow on the right of the Quick Access Toolbar and choose Minimize the Ribbon.

# Choose menu commands

Office 2007 has done away with the familiar series of menus (File, Edit, Format, Tools and so on) arranged horizontally across the top of an application window. Instead, you'll find menus that drop down when you click the Office button, the Quick Access toolbar and the Mini-toolbar. The same menus you may have grown used to are all there – you just have to look in different places to find them.

## To use the Office menu

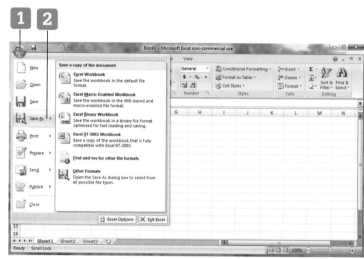

**1** Click the Office button.

**2** Click the command of your choice. If you see a right arrow next to the menu command, point to the arrow to display a submenu with further options, then choose the one you want.

## To use a shortcut menu

**3** Right-click a cell in a spreadsheet, paragraph or graphic.

**4** Choose a command in the shortcut menu that pops up. If you see an arrow next to the context menu command, point to the arrow and choose the more specific command on the submenu that appears.

 **HOT TIP:** You can also open a shortcut menu by right-clicking a cell or icon in the program you're working with.

# Work with toolbars

Office 2007, like previous versions, lets you choose toolbar buttons and other commands. Some of the most common commands, including Save and Undo, are found on the Quick Access Toolbar. The Quick Access Toolbar is the most obvious of Office 2007's toolbars – it is always found at the top of the current application window, unless you have customised its settings. Other toolbars are found on the Ribbon and act just as those in previous versions of Office.

## Choose a toolbar or Ribbon command

1 Pass your mouse over a toolbar button to display a ScreenTip explaining what it does.

2 Click the button to execute the command or click the dropdown arrow next to the button and choose a command or option.

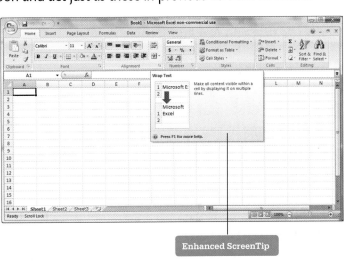

Enhanced ScreenTip

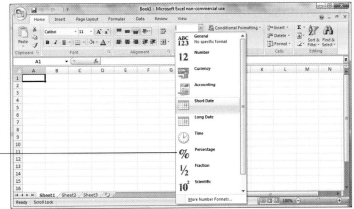

Dropdown list menu

**DID YOU KNOW?**

You can turn ScreenTips on or off by clicking the Office button, clicking <Program> Options, clicking the ScreenTip Scheme dropdown list, choosing Don't Show ScreenTips, then clicking OK.

# Manage the Quick Access Toolbar

The Quick Access Toolbar – new to Office 2007 – is worth exploring in detail because it allows you to make your most frequently chosen command buttons or groups readily available. Those commands can be ones that are normally hard to find or at least take several mouse clicks to execute. You can also move the toolbar below or above the Ribbon so that you can find it more easily.

### Delete a toolbar button

1 Click the Customize Quick Access Toolbar down arrow at the far right of the toolbar.

2 Click one of the ticked items on the dropdown list (only ticked items are shown in the toolbar).

### Add a toolbar button

Do one of the following.

3 Right-click the command you want to add and choose Add to Quick Access Toolbar. Click the Customize Quick Access Toolbar dropdown list arrow.

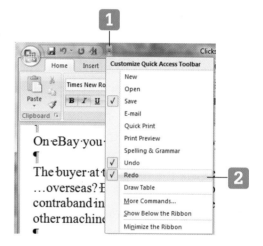

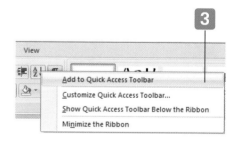

**HOT TIP:** You can move the Quick Access Toolbar by clicking the Customize Quick Access Toolbar down arrow, then choosing Show Below the Ribbon or Show Above the Ribbon.

**4** If you don't see the command that you want to add, click the Customize Quick Access Toolbar down arrow and choose More Commands.

**5** Click the command you want to add.

**6** Click Add.

**7** When you have finished adding commands, click OK.

**? DID YOU KNOW?**

If you have added many commands to the Quick Access Toolbar and it has become unwieldy, you can restore it to its normal state. Click the Office button, choose <Program> Options, click Customize, then click Reset. Click OK to close the Options dialogue box.

# Customise the Quick Access Toolbar

The Customize tab in the Options dialogue box appears when you choose More Commands from the Quick Access Toolbar's dropdown list menu. This dialogue box includes options that let you identify all of the command buttons and menu options in your Office program. If nothing else, it's useful to scan the list to see all the options you have – you're likely to find some that you never knew existed.

1 Click the Choose commands from list arrow and choose Popular Commands, All Commands or pick commands from a specific Ribbon.

2 Choose For all documents if you want the commands to be available on the Quick Access Toolbar for all documents/spreadsheets/presentations you create with your Office program of choice. Choose For <document name> if you want the command to be available only in the current document.

3 Click the Move Up or Move Down buttons to change the order of buttons.

4 Click OK.

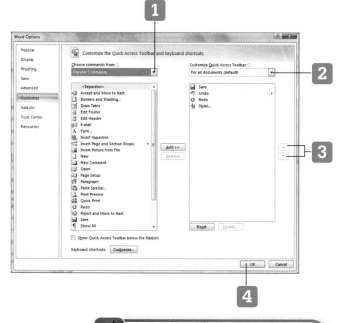

**HOT TIP:** You can separate each button by clicking <Separator> and then clicking Add. This places a line between the buttons.

# Choose dialogue box options

Dialogue boxes are indispensable parts of every Office application. They present you with specific options and commands for many functions – sizes of fonts, table formats and much more. The level of organisation in the Ribbon means that some dialogue boxes are accessed differently from previous versions of Office. Office 2007's enhanced ToolTips, however, let you know when a dialogue box is available and even give you previews of what they look like.

1 Pass your mouse pointer over the arrow that points down and to the right if you see one at the bottom of a tool group in the Ribbon to display the ToolTip.

2 Click the button to open the dialogue box.

3 If the dialogue box is divided into separate tabs, click the one that contains the controls you want.

4 Choose the commands you want.

5 Click OK.

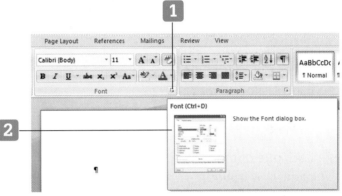

**HOT TIP:** Press the Tab key to move from one field to another in a dialogue box to save you having to use your mouse or touchpad to move around. Press Shift+Tab to move backwards.

**HOT TIP:** Many dialogue boxes contain a preview area that lets you see how text or other elements will be formatted based on your selections.

# Use the status bar

28

The status bar is the area at the very bottom of an Office window. Often, the status bar displays useful information about the current file (Word, for instance, gives you a word count in the lower left-hand corner, but in most Office applications, the lower right-hand controls are the same: they give you different ways of viewing the current document, and they enable you to zoom in or out.

**1** Pass your mouse arrow over one of the page view options in Word, Excel or PowerPoint to display the relevant ToolTip.

**2** Click one of the page view options to change the view.

**3** Click the plus or minus signs to zoom in or out by one percentage point at a time.

**4** Move the slider to the left or right to change the view.

**5** Click and drag the resize handle to change the size of the window.

Click to add header

# Add or remove status bar contents

**1** Right-click the status bar and choose an unticked item to add it to the status bar.

**2** Right-click the status bar and choose a ticked item to remove it from the status bar.

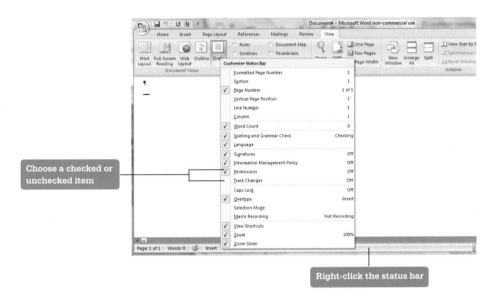

Choose a checked or unchecked item

Right-click the status bar

**? DID YOU KNOW?**

The status bar can display the name of the current Office theme. The status bar also lets you see whether certain features are on or off, including Signatures, Permissions, Caps Lock, Num Lock and many more.

# Change task panes

A task pane is a subdivision of the main Office program window. Task panes appear when they are needed or when you click the appropriate dialogue box launcher icon. For instance the arrows next to Clipboard and Clip Art in the Ribbon each open task panes with controls related to them. Task panes can be resized and there is usually a Close button (an X) in the upper right-hand corner so that you can close them when you're done. A related subdivision of the Office window, a window pane, is a part of a single window, such as a window that has been split into two sections.

**1** Click the Clipboard arrow or another dialogue box launcher icon to open a task pane.

**2** Click the down arrow to move or close the task pane.

**3** Click the item displayed in the pane to select and work with it.

**4** Click the Options button to view options for the task pane.

**5** If necessary, use the scroll bars to locate Windows Photo Gallery.

**6** Click Windows Photo Gallery to open the application.

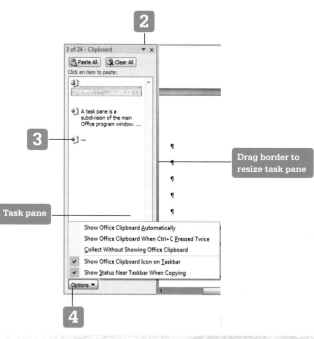

Drag border to resize task pane

Task pane

**?  DID YOU KNOW?**

To open a window pane, do one of two things: either click and drag the Split button (which appears as a horizontal line at the top of the scroll bar) or click the View tab and click the Split button in the Window tool group.

# Manage multiple windows

My daughters are always amazed at the number of applications and windows I have open at any one time. The fact is that I need to be doing several things at once and chances are you do, too.

If you need to work with multiple document windows, you'll work faster and will be able to switch from one file to another more quickly if you arrange them efficiently. In other words you don't need to fill your computer screen with a single window, you can display several windows at once and switch back and forth, making each one active as you need to work with it. Each window contains its own Ribbon and work area.

## Resize or move a window

1 Click the title bar of an inactive window to make it active.

2 Click one of the buttons in the upper right-hand corner to manipulate window size:

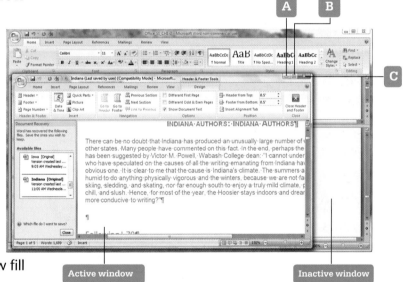

**A** Maximize button: click this button to make the window fill the screen.

Active window   Inactive window

**B** Restore Down button: if you have maximised a window and want to restore it to its previous smaller size, click this button.

**C** Close button: Click here to close the window.

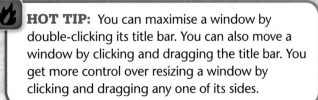

**HOT TIP:** You can maximise a window by double-clicking its title bar. You can also move a window by clicking and dragging the title bar. You get more control over resizing a window by clicking and dragging any one of its sides.

## Arrange multiple windows

**1** Open all the documents that you want to work with.

**2** Click the View tab on the active document.

**3** In the Window tool group, do one of the following:

- Click Arrange All and choose an option (Tiled, Horizontal, Vertical or Cascade) and click OK

- Click Switch Windows, then choose the document you want to work with

- Click New Window to open a new window that contains the contents of the current document.

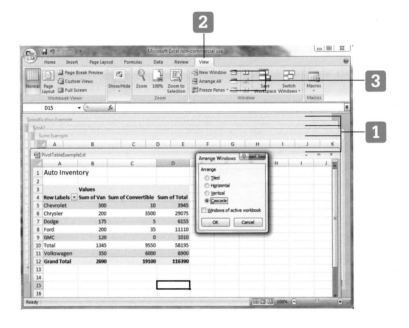

**ALERT:** In order for the Reset Window feature to work, you must first have chosen the View Side by Side option.

## Arrange windows side by side

**1** Open the two Word or Excel documents that you want to compare.

**2** Click the View tab in the Ribbon.

**3** In the Window tool group, do one of the following:

- Click View Side by Side if you want to view the two files vertically at the same time

- Click Synchronous Scrolling to synchronise the two open files so that, when you scroll one, the other scrolls along with it (this is a great way to scan and compare the contents of two files)

- Click Reset Window Position to reset the window position of the two files so that they share an equal amount of the screen.

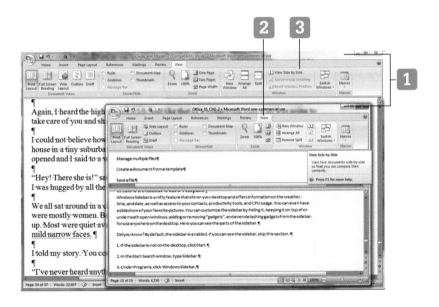

# Create a document from a template

You don't need to create a new document from scratch. Office 2007 gives you a selection of professionally designed templates that you can use as a starting point. Templates work well when you know what your content will be but you don't have the time or experience to create a look and feel for presenting it in its best light. A template gives you colours, type styles and other attributes – you only need to add text and graphics. The New dialogue box lets you choose one of the templates that comes with Office or pick one from an online library at Microsoft Office Online's website.

**1** Click the Office button and choose New.

**2** When the New Document window opens, do one of the following:

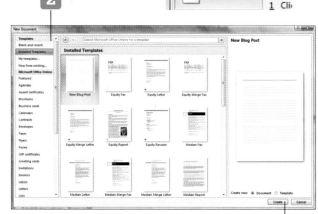

- Choose Blank and recent from the Templates list to open recently used templates

- Click Installed Templates and choose a template that comes with Office

- Click My templates to choose any templates that you have created and saved

- Click Featured, then choose a template from the Spotlight section

- Click a Microsoft Office Online template category, then choose a template from the online list.

**3** Click Create or Download.

**4** If necessary, click the template of your choice and click OK.

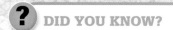

---

**? DID YOU KNOW?**

Templates have been created by third parties and made available on Microsoft Office Online's website. Go to www.microsoft.com, click Office and search for Office Templates.

# Save a file

Saving a document, in any Office application, probably seems simple: click Office and choose Save, or press the Save button in the Home tab of the Ribbon. But you have many other options at your disposal for saving files in different formats. You need to choose Save As, rather than Save, the first time you save a file or if you want to save the file with a different name. When you save a file, make sure you save it in the desired format. Office 2007 files are saved in a format based on XML (eXtensible Markup Language). You can also save in compatibility mode, which creates files in Office 97-2003 format (in other words, the document can be opened in Office 97 up to Office 2003).

## Save a file in Office 2007 format

1 Click the Office button.

2 Choose Save As.

3 Click the Save in list arrow and identify the folder or drive you want to save the file to.

4 Type a file name for your document in the File name box.

5 Click the Save as type dropdown list and choose the file format for your file.

6 Click the Authors or Tags fields and type properties information about the file.

7 When you are done, click Save.

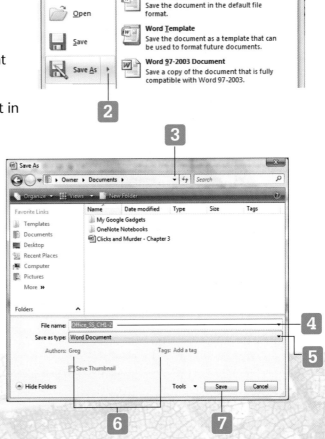

## Save in Office 97-2003 format

**1** If the open file is already in Office 97-2003 format, simply click the Save button on the Quick Access Toolbar, press Ctrl+S or click the Office button and choose Save.

**2** If the open file is in Office 2007 or another format, Click the Office button, choose Save As and choose <Program> 97-2003 Document.

## Specify save defaults

**3** Click the Office button, and click the <Program> Options button.

**4** Click Save.

**5** Choose the save options: pick a default save format from the dropdown list and a default file location.

**6** Click OK.

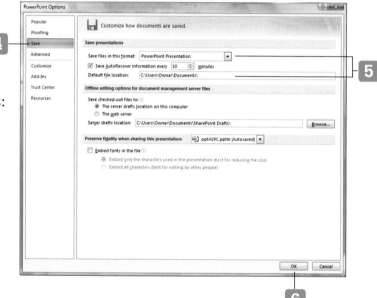

### WHAT DOES THIS MEAN?

**XML** The eXtensible Markup Language format results in smaller file sizes and enhanced file recovery compared with other formats.

**Compatibility mode**: Good if you are sharing the file with others who don't have Office 2007, but it disables new Office 2007 features that can't be handled by earlier versions.

# Save an Office file in a different format

One of the biggest advantages of using Office 2007 is the ability to save a file created in one format in another. Also, because Office 2007 presents you with an integrated series of applications, that means you can save a file created in one application (such as Word) in another format (such as PowerPoint). It means, too, that you can save a file as a Web page, so you can view it online with a Web browser. Excel also has a selection of specialised file formats, such as the binary file format BIFF12, which is optimal for large, complex workbooks.

**1** Click the Office button, choose Save As, then choose Other Formats.

**2** Click the Save as type dropdown list and choose the file format you want. Some possible formats are listed in Table 1.1.

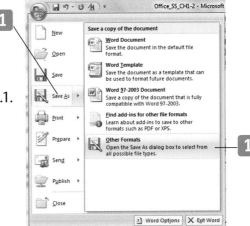

**Table 1.1 Office 2007 Save as type formats**

| Save as type | File extension | Used with |
| --- | --- | --- |
| Word document | .docx | Word 2007 files |
| Excel workbook | .xlsx | Excel 2007 workbooks |
| PowerPoint presentation | .pptx | PowerPoint 2007 presentations |
| Access 2007 database | .accdb | Access 2007 databases |
| Excel 97-2003 workbook | .xls | Excel 97-2003 workbooks |
| PowerPoint 97-2003 | .ppt | PowerPoint 97-2003 presentations |
| PowerPoint show | .pps, .ppsx | Point Point 2007 slide show |
| Access 2002-2003 database | .mdb | Access 2002-2004 database |
| Portable Document Format (PDF) | .pdf | Adobe PDF format |
| Web page | .htm, .html | Web page folder containing an .htm file |
| Single-file Web page | .mht, .mhtml | A single Web page .htm file |

# Find Help while you're working

Office 2007's Help utility is more than just a database of articles designed to help you use an application more effectively. It also connects you to Microsoft Office Online, where you can seamlessly search the Web for answers to your questions. You can search the Help utility by keyword or phrase or else browse by topic. When you search, you are presented with a list of possible answers, with the most likely one or the most frequently used one positioned at the top of the list.

**1** Click the Help button, the blue question mark near the top of the Ribbon.

**2** Find the Help topic you need by:

- Clicking a Help category on the home page, then clicking a specific topic

- Clicking the Table of Contents button, clicking a category, then clicking a topic.

**3** Read the topic to find out more, clicking links to get more information.

**4** Navigate the Help files by clicking the toolbar buttons Back, Forward, Stop, Refresh and Home much like a Web browser.

**5** Click Keep On Top to keep the Help window on top of other open windows. When Keep On Top is selected, the button changes to Not On Top to keep it behind other windows.

**6** Click Close when you're done.

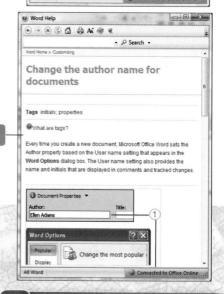

**? DID YOU KNOW?**

To search the Help database, open the Help button by pressing F1 or clicking the Help icon. Then click the dropdown arrow next to the Search button on the Help window's toolbar. Then select the location where you want to search. Type one or more keywords in the text box next to the Search button, then click the Search button itself. You can then scan the list of topics to find the information you want.

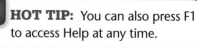
**HOT TIP:** You can also press F1 to access Help at any time.

# Change preferences

You are already familiar with the <Program> Options window from preceding tasks in this chapter. It's the place where you can change how you want the application to save files, display information and handle specialised tasks. The Word Options window contains commands that control proofing, for instance, while the Excel Options window contains plenty of options for handling formulas. By setting preferences, you save time as you tell the program how to perform frequently used functions upfront, so that you don't have to do it repeatedly later on.

**1** Click Start and click the <Program> Options button.

**2** When the <Program> Options window opens, click one of the categories in the left-hand column to see what sorts of preferences you can set.

**3** Click Popular to view frequently used controls, such as the option to display the Developer tab in the Ribbon.

**4** Click a specialised heading to view controls that are specific to the program.

**5** When you're done, click OK.

# Change views

If you use Word frequently for word processing, you're probably aware that the program gives you a variety of ways to view information. These include Normal, Page Layout and Print Layout. Don't stick with the default view – at least take a moment to look over the view options available, to see how you can view information. Some of the views are new to Office 2007 and, even if you've used Office programs before, you won't be familiar with these.

**1** Click the View tab.

**2** Look over the buttons in the Document Views group and click each one in turn to view your available options:

- **Word:** Print Layout, Full Screen Reading, Web Layout, Outline and Draft

- **Excel**: Normal, Page Layout and Page Break Preview

- **PowerPoint**: Normal, Slide Sorter and Slide Show

- **Access**: Form, Datasheet, Layout, Design and PivotTable.

**? DID YOU KNOW?**
You can also use the view buttons on the View tab in the Ribbon to switch between views. The View Selector buttons on the right side of the status bar, near the zoom controls, also let you switch quickly between views.

**ALERT:** If you use the View tab, you won't see view options for Access. You need to use the View Selector to switch between views for this application.

# Update Office from the Web

Microsoft periodically releases software updates that improve the stability and security of particular applications or the suite as a whole. Each program in the suite gives you a way to manually connect to the Microsoft Update website so your system can be scanned for any needed updates. You'll then have the chance to choose which updates you actually want to install.

**1** Click Office, then click <Program> Options.

**2** Click Resources.

**3** Click Check for Updates.

**4** Click Install updates.

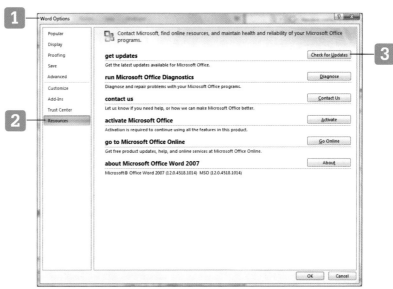

**ALERT:** In Outlook or Publisher, you need to open Help (press F1), then click Check for updates.

# Close a file and exit Office

Those of us who have lost information because we didn't save it or experienced slowdowns because too many files were open know the importance of saving and closing files when we've finished working on them. When you're done working on it, close the file. Closing doesn't mean that you quit the Office application altogether – you just free up memory so that you can work on other files. Once you've completed your work, you can exit Office completely.

## Close an Office file

**1** Do one of the following:

- Click the Office button and choose Close

- Click the Close button, the X in the upper right-hand corner of the window.

**2** Save the file when prompted.

## Exit an Office application

**3** Do one of the following:

- Click the Office button and click Exit <Program>

- Click the Close box in the corner of all open windows.

**4** Click the Save button in the Quick Access Toolbar if prompted.

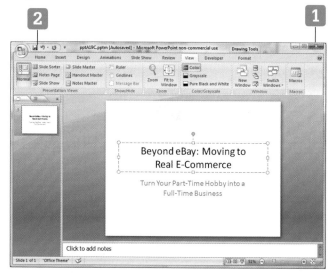

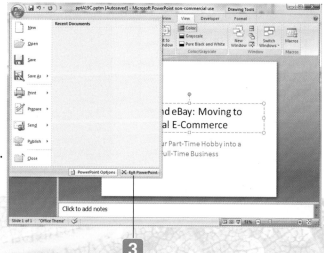

# 2 Working with text

# Introduction

Text is an important part of every Office application, is central to Word and is an integral part of PowerPoint as well. The most fundamental aspects of working with text – typing, copying, cutting, pasting and spell checking – apply to all Office applications. Once you learn how to do the basics in one program, you can apply what you've learned to the others as well.

Office contains plenty of built-in functions that let you go well beyond the basics. The Find and Replace utility, which is found in nearly every Office application, is especially robust. Spellchecking can go well beyond simply notifying you if a word has a typo in it – you can use Office to suggest the right words and help you with your grammar as well.

# Select text

Even users who work with text on a regular basis (like me) are unfamiliar with all of the tricks for selecting text. All of the Office applications give you shortcuts that make it easy to select words, sentences, paragraphs or lines. It's worth going through all of the selection options at least once so you can be aware that they exist. Then, even if you use the same selection options (such as double-clicking or clicking and dragging) over and over, you'll surely find occasions when a special keyboard shortcut or other trick will save time and improve your productivity.

## Use the mouse

1  To select a word or phrase, drag the mouse over it (that is, click at the beginning of the text, hold the mouse down and move along to the end), then release the mouse and the word or phrase will be shaded to show that you have selected it.

2  If you want to select a whole line or paragraph, move the pointer to the left of the text until it points to the right, then click to select a line, or double-click to select the whole of that paragraph.

3  To select the entire document, again while the pointer is pointing to the right, triple-click.

4  Alternatively, press Ctrl, then click anywhere in a sentence to select it.

5  You can also triple-click anywhere in a paragraph to select it.

6  To select a vertical column of numbers or text, press Alt and drag the mouse arrow down and to the right over the text.

Make sure mouse points to right

## Use keyboard shortcuts

If you don't want to use a
mouse (or don't have one
available), you can select
characters, words or longer
text segments by using one of
the keyboard shortcuts shown
in Table 2.1.

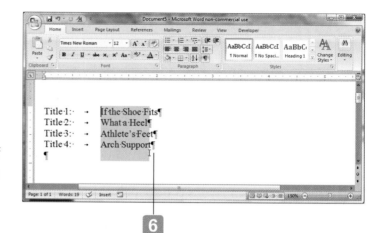

**6**

## Table 2.1 Text selection keyboard shortcuts

| To select this | Use this keyboard combination |
| --- | --- |
| One character to the right | Press Shift+right arrow |
| One character to the left | Press Shift+left arrow |
| One line down from the current line | Press End, then press Shift+down arrow |
| One line up from the current line | Press Home, then press Shift+up arrow |
| An entire document, from the end to the start | Position the cursor at the end and press Ctrl+Shift+Home |
| An entire document, from the start to the end | Position the cursor at the beginning and press Ctrl+Shift+End |
| An entire document | Press Ctrl+A |
| A word, sentence, paragraph or document | Press F8 once to enter selection mode, then press F8 once to select a word, twice to select a sentence, three times to select a paragraph or four times to select the entire file. Press Esc to cancel selection mode. |

# Edit text

Once you have learned to select the text you want, as described in the preceding task, you can edit the text so it looks and reads the way that you want. Most of the time, that means you'll want to cut, copy or paste text from one location to another. You can use keyboard commands for any of those functions, but you can also use a mouse to drag and drop, copying or moving text from one file to another or from one location to another in the same file.

## Select and edit text

**1** Use one of the techniques described in the preceding task or drag the text cursor over the text you want to select. The text is highlighted to indicate that it has been selected.

**2** Then, do one of the following:

* type your new text to immediately replace the highlighted text

* press Backspace or Delete (Del) to delete the text and then type the new text.

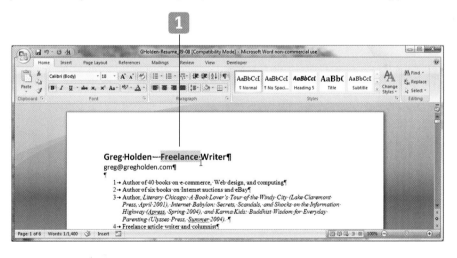

**?** **DID YOU KNOW?**

You can double-click a word to select it or triple-click a paragraph to select it (see Table 2.1 for more suggestions).

## Drag and drop text

**1** Make sure that the text you want to move and the destination point are *both* visible on the screen. This may mean opening two files or displaying them side by side.

**2** Select the text that you want to copy or move by pointing your mouse arrow at the text, then clicking and holding down the mouse button.

**3** Drag the selected text to the new location, then release the mouse button (and keyboard, if necessary).

**4** Click elsewhere in the file to deselect the text.

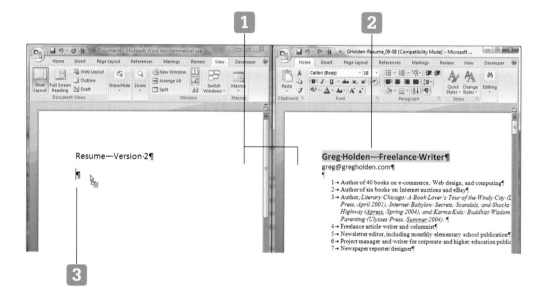

**HOT TIP:** If you want to *copy* text, while pointing at it, press and hold down Ctrl while clicking and holding down the mouse. A plus sign (+) appears, which indicates that you are dragging a copy of the text, not the original.

**SEE ALSO:** See Manage multiple windows in Chapter 1 for instructions on how to arrange two documents next to one another.

# Copy and move text

As you learned in the previous task, copying is different from moving. When you move text (or an image or other object), nothing remains in the original location afterwards. When you copy, however, you leave the original in its previous location and take a copy of it to the new one.

Another difference is that, when you copy, a duplicate of what you have copied is placed on the Clipboard. The Clipboard can hold several items, not just one. You can use the Paste Special command to control exactly what you want to paste into the new location.

1. Select the text that you want to copy.

2. Click the Copy or Cut button on the Home tab.

3. Click to position the cursor at the location where you want to paste the text.

4. Click Paste or press Ctrl+V.

5. To control the way you paste the text, click the Paste Options button and choose an option from the dropdown menu.

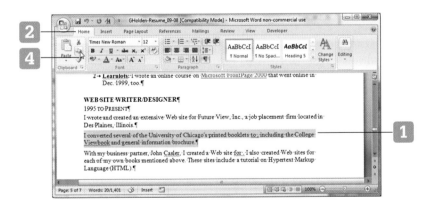

## WHAT DOES THIS MEAN?

**Marquee**: A rectangle made up of dashes that seems to be blinking or moving in some way.

## ? DID YOU KNOW?

When you paste text (or data) in Excel, a marquee appears around the pasted data until you press Esc.

When you paste text (or data), it remains on the Clipboard, so you can paste it again if you need to.

# Use the Office Clipboard task pane

Usually, the Clipboard is something that you don't see, but it acts as an invisible receptacle for text and other content you've placed there so you can paste it elsewhere. You can see the items on the Clipboard, however, and choose them by clicking the Clipboard dialogue box launcher and opening the Clipboard as a task pane.

1. Click the Home tab if necessary.

2. Click the Clipboard dialogue box launcher.

3. Click the text you want to copy.

4. Click Copy. The content is added to the Clipboard task pane.

5. Position the cursor where you want to paste the text.

6. Click the dropdown arrow next to the clipboard item and choose Paste.

7. Click the task pane's Close button to close it.

## Use the Paste Special dialogue box

8. Click the down arrow beneath the Paste button.

9. Choose Paste Special.

10. Choose the format you want for the text or other content to be pasted.

11. Click OK.

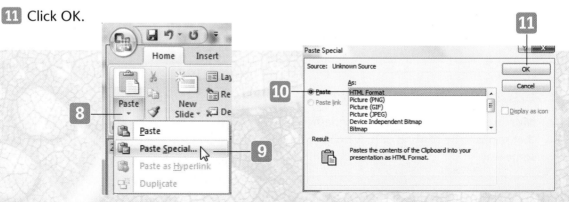

# Find and replace text

The Find and Replace utility is present throughout Office's applications. Though the exact commands differ from one program to another, the basic purpose is the same. The Find dialogue box lets you find text, while the Replace dialogue box lets you replace it with different text. You also have the option of searching up, down, or throughout a file, or to find whole words or text with certain formatting.

## Find text

**1** Position the cursor at the start of the document or at the point from which you want the search to begin. Click the Home tab, if necessary.

**2** Click the Find button and choose Find from the dropdown list.

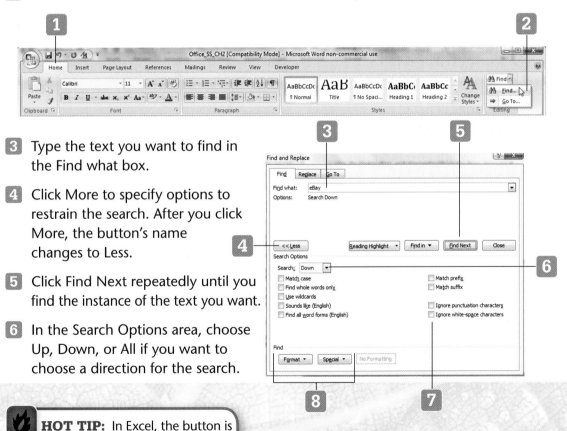

**3** Type the text you want to find in the Find what box.

**4** Click More to specify options to restrain the search. After you click More, the button's name changes to Less.

**5** Click Find Next repeatedly until you find the instance of the text you want.

**6** In the Search Options area, choose Up, Down, or All if you want to choose a direction for the search.

**HOT TIP:** In Excel, the button is called Find & Select.

**7** Click the options in the Search Options area to search for whole words only or impose other constraints.

**8** Click in the Find area and choose from the Format or Special lists to find only text that has specific formatting.

## If you use Excel...

**9** Click Find All to find all instances of a formula or cell reference in a worksheet.

**10** Results appear in the box below this button.

## Replace text

**11** Click at the beginning of the file or at the point in the file where you want to start replacing text.

**12** Click the Home tab if necessary.

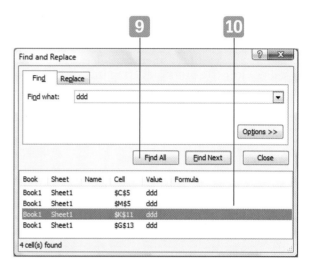

**13** Click Replace or Find and Replace, depending on the program you are using. The Find and Replace dialogue box opens with the Replace tab in front.

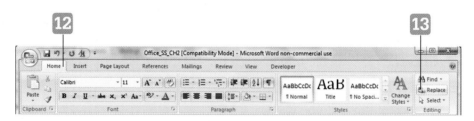

**14** Type the text that you want to find in the Find what box.

**15** Type the replacement text in the Replace with box.

**16** Click Find Next to find the first instance of the specified text.

**17** Click Replace to replace the first instance only or Replace All to replace all instances at once.

**18** Click Close when the message box appears to show that you have reached the end of the document.

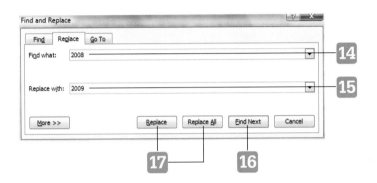

**DID YOU KNOW?**

Find and Replace doesn't just work with text. You can also use it to locate and correct formulas or references to cell numbers.

**HOT TIP:** If you are searching for one specific instance of a word or phrase, keep clicking Find Next until it appears. You don't have to replace text if you simply click Find Next.

# Correct text automatically

The AutoCorrect feature you have probably noticed in Word is available for other Office applications, too. AutoCorrect automatically repairs spelling or grammar errors as you type. It is helpful as it is, but becomes more powerful when you customise the application's dictionary to include special terms, such as proper names or brand names. You can also configure AutoCorrect to automatically add symbols, such as the trademark ™ symbol when you type the letters TM, for instance.

## Activate AutoCorrect

**1** Click the Office button.

**2** Choose <Program> Options.

**3** Click Proofing.

**4** Click AutoCorrect Options.

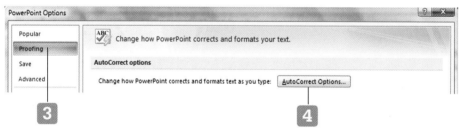

**? DID YOU KNOW?**

When AutoCorrect fixes a word, a tiny blue box appears under the first letter. Pass your mouse arrow over the box and the AutoCorrect Options dialogue box appears so that you can control whether or not you want the word corrected or change other AutoCorrect settings.

**5** Click the box next to Show AutoCorrect Options buttons to display the blue button that lets you change AutoCorrect options.

**6** Make sure Replace text as you type is ticked.

**7** Select the capitalisation corrections you want AutoCorrect to make.

**8** If you want to specify exceptions that AutoCorrect should not change, click here.

**9** Click OK.

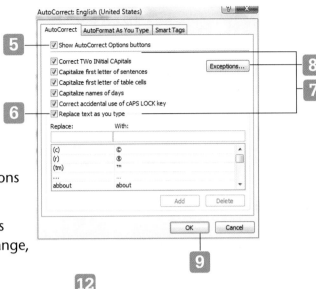

### Modify an AutoCorrect entry

**10** Click the Office button and click <Program> Options.

**11** Click Proofing and then click AutoCorrect.

**12** Click the AutoCorrect tab if necessary.

**13** If you want to add a misspelled word to the dictionary, type the misspelled word in the Replace box and the replacement in the With box, then click Add.

**14** To edit the dictionary, select an item in it and click Delete or type the replacement.

**15** Click OK.

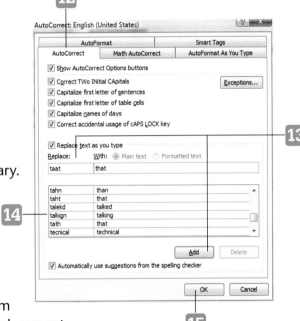

# Check spelling and grammar

As you learned in the preceding text, Office's AutoCorrect function has the ability to check your text as you type. You can also run manual spellchecks to make sure that your documents are free of misspellings.

The spellchecker is available in all Office programs. You can check the spelling as you're working on the file or when you've reached the end.

### Check spelling manually

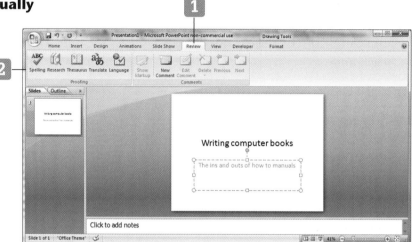

1 Click the Review tab.

2 Click Spelling. (In Word, click Spelling and Grammar.)

3 If a 'the spelling check is complete' message appears, click OK.

4 If the Spelling or Spelling and Grammar dialogue box appears, do one or more of the following:

- Click Ignore Once to skip the word once

- Click Ignore All or Ignore Rule to skip every instance of the term

- Click Add to Dictionary to add the word to your Office dictionary so that it won't show up as misspelled in future

**HOT TIP:** In Outlook, click the Message tab in a Message window. In Access, click the Home tab to find the Spelling button.

- Click one of the words given in the Suggestions box if you want to use it as a replacement, then click Change or Change All

- Click AutoCorrect to add the corrected word (the word you have selected in the Suggestions list) to the AutoCorrect list.

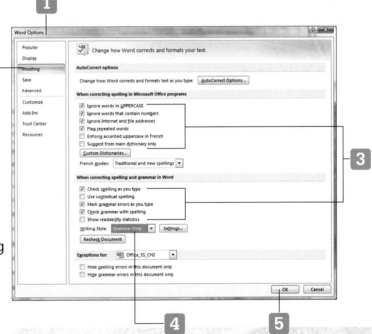

5  Click Resume if you have stopped the spellcheck or Close when you have finished.

## Change spelling and grammar options

1  Click the Office button and click <Program> Options.

2  Click Proofing.

3  Select or clear the spelling and grammar options by clicking on the boxes to tick or untick them.

4  Choose Grammar and Style from the dropdown list by Writing Style to choose style as well as words.

5  Click OK.

---

**?  DID YOU KNOW?**

Word's Spelling and Grammar function reports sentences or phrases that are problematic as well as words it thinks are misspelled. You don't have to do anything special to check grammar – just follow the steps given for checking your spelling in order to make changes or ignore suggestions given regarding grammar.

# Consult the thesaurus

The Review tab available in all Office applications not only lets you check your spelling, it can also suggest words for you. It's a function that you might not even know Office can perform until you really need it. Say you're searching for the right word and you can't find your printed thesaurus – instead of scratching your head and guessing, use the built-in thesaurus you already have in your computer.

## Use the context menu

**1** Right-click the word you want to find a synonym for.

**2** Choose one of the following from the context menu:

- Synonyms to choose one of a few synonyms Office suggests for you

- Look Up to look up the word in the thesaurus.

**3** You can also choose Thesaurus from the submenu to look up other options.

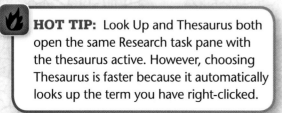

**HOT TIP:** Look Up and Thesaurus both open the same Research task pane with the thesaurus active. However, choosing Thesaurus is faster because it automatically looks up the term you have right-clicked.

## Use the Research task pane

**1** Highlight the text you want to look up. Click the Review tab.

**2** Click the Research button.

**3** Click the list arrow and choose a thesaurus from the list if you want to use a special thesaurus.

**4** Point to one of the words found in the thesaurus.

**5** Click the list arrow that appears next to the word and choose one of the following:

- Insert to replace the highlighted word with this new one

- Copy to copy the new word to the Clipboard so that you can paste it

- Look Up to look up the word.

**6** When you've finished, click the Close box in the Research task pane.

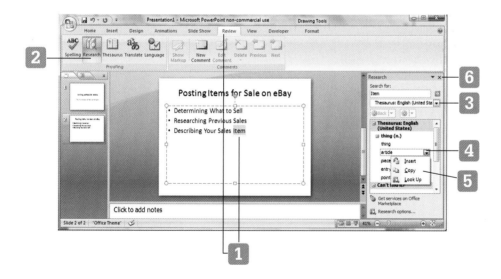

---

**HOT TIP:** In Outlook, click the Message tab in a Message window, then click the Spelling button, to access the thesaurus.

**? DID YOU KNOW?**
You can install thesauruses in other languages by looking under Research Options in the Research task pane.

# Create text boxes

Another way to insert text is to add it to a shape. If you use the drawing tools available in Office applications to draw simple shapes such as rectangles, circles or triangles, you can add text to those shapes. The text can serve as a label so that the reader understands what is being shown. You can do this by simply typing the text within the shape or else inserting a text box.

**1** Click the shape to select it.

**2** Click the Insert tab.

**3** Click Text Box.

**4** Click one of the text box styles. Click Draw Text Box if you want to control the size and position of the text box precisely.

**5** Click the dashed line around the text and drag it to reposition the text.

**6** Click inside the text box to position the cursor so that you can edit the text inside.

**7** To format the text box (for instance, to change the border or add a fill colour), right-click inside it and choose Format Text Box.

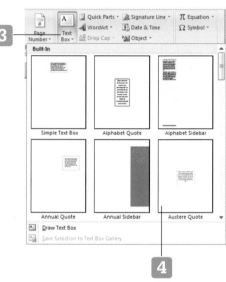

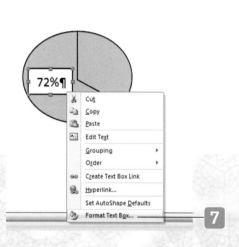

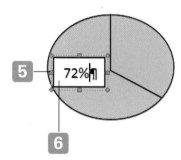

**? DID YOU KNOW?**

When you place text inside a shape, it becomes part of the shape. So, if you rotate or otherwise modify the shape, the text in it is modified as well.

# Translate text

In the previous task, when you right-clicked a word, you might have noticed the word Translate as one of the options in the context menu. Office can translate text into one of a few languages for you. As you might expect, using a computer to translate from one language to another is never as good as having a human being do so, but, in a pinch, it can help if the word you're working on is simple.

1. Highlight the term.
2. Click Review.
3. Click Translate to open the Research task pane.
4. Choose a different language from the options under To.
5. Enter the word you want translated in the Search for box at the top of the task pane.
6. Read the suggestions for translation given at the bottom of the task pane.

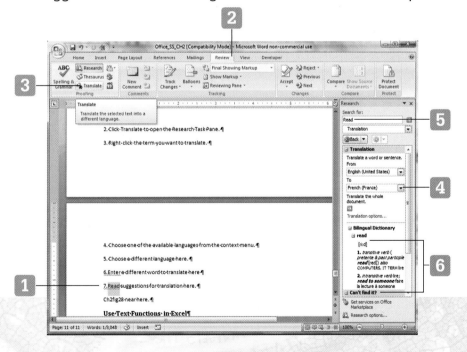

# Import text files

If you want to go beyond simply cutting and pasting text and add an entire file to another Office document (for instance, a PowerPoint presentation), you can import the file.

**1** Click the Office button.

**2** Click Open.

**3** Click the Files of type dropdown list arrow and choose Text Files.

**4** Click the text file you want to import.

**5** Click Open.

**6** If a File Conversion dialogue box opens, click an encoding option.

**7** Click OK.

# Insert a symbol

If you ever want to add an em dash (—), a pounds symbol (£) or a trademark symbol (™), you can do it quickly from any Office application. You can choose from a brief list of the most popular symbols in the Symbol dropdown list or open the Symbol dialogue box to find a complete list of options.

**1** Click to position the text cursor at the spot in the document where you want to insert the symbol.

**2** Click the Insert tab.

**3** Click the Symbol dropdown list.

**4** Click the symbol you want from the selection.

**5** If you don't see the symbol you want, click the Symbol button at the bottom left of the dropdown list to open the Symbol dialogue box. You can also click More Symbols to open the Symbol dialogue box.

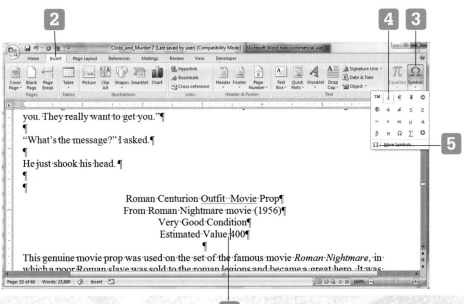

**6** Click the Font dropdown list arrow to choose a new font if you want to view new symbols.

**7** Click the symbol or character you want.

**8** Click Insert.

**9** Click the Special Characters tab to add em dashes and other common symbols.

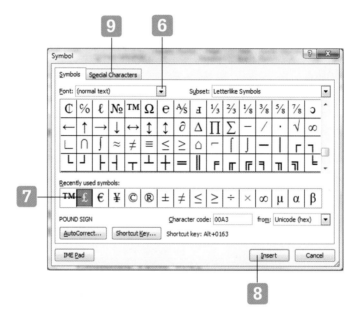

**? DID YOU KNOW?**

If you don't see the symbol you want in the Symbols dialogue box, you can choose a different font from the Font list and try again. Different fonts contain different ranges of symbols.

**HOT TIP:** Scan the list of Recently used symbols at the bottom of the Symbols dialogue box to quickly add the one you want without having to look for it.

# Load a custom dictionary

A custom dictionary lets you look up the meanings of words in foreign languages. You can also create your own custom dictionary if you have a large number of special terms that you use regularly.

Before you can add a custom dictionary, you need to enable it using the Custom Dictionaries dialogue box. One particularly nice aspect of using custom dictionaries is the fact that any changes you make to them are shared with all of your other Microsoft Office programs.

**1** Click the Office Button and choose <Program>Options.

**2** Click Proofing.

**3** Click Custom Dictionaries.

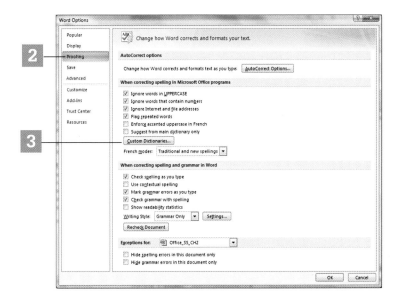

4 Tick the box next to CUSTOM.DIC (Default) in the All Languages box.

5 Click the Dictionary language dropdown list arrow and choose a language for your new custom dictionary.

6 Choose options to create your dictionary or add an existing one:

- Edit Word List – click here to add, cut or edit terms

- Change Default – click to select a new default dictionary

- New – click to create a new dictionary

- Add – click here to insert an existing dictionary

- Remove – click to remove a dictionary.

7 Click OK when you've finished, and OK to close <Program> Options.

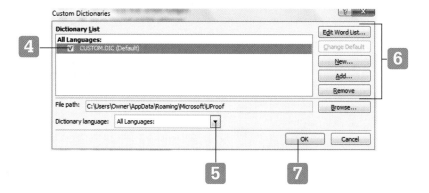

# 3 Working with art and photos

# Introduction

As they say, a picture is worth a thousand words – or cells in a spreadsheet or pages in a presentation. Illustrations and photos make your content more compelling, no matter what program you're using. Microsoft Office doesn't include a graphics program as such, but each of its component applications gives you the ability to add and edit visual elements that make your information more compelling. On top of that, Office provides you with an extensive library of clip art – drawings and photos that have been created by professional artists which you are free to add to your files. Office also gives you links to help you search through additional clip art collections on the Web.

Once you add a picture, you can resize, compress or crop it using simple drawing tools that are included on a drawing toolbar. This toolbar also enables you to create your own diagrams and illustrations from scratch. In addition, you have the option of adding WordArt – text that comes in colourful and creative fonts, which you can stretch into imaginative shapes and styles. All of these graphic tools are intended to make your documents more interesting with a minimum of effort. Explore them and your work will be more interesting and more readable as well.

# Browse Office clip art

Whenever you want to add an illustration to break up text or boost the attractiveness of a document, consider looking in Office's clip art files before you start taking photos or scanning images. Office comes with built-in clip art that you can add to your documents for free. What's more, you can browse the Office clip art files from within the application itself rather than having to open a separate graphics program. You can search the files by keyword to find what you need more easily.

**1** Click the Insert tab.

**2** Click the Clip Art button.

**3** When the Clip Art task pane opens, type a keyword in the Search for box.

**4** Click Go.

**5** Click the Search in and Results should be boxes and choose options to narrow your search.

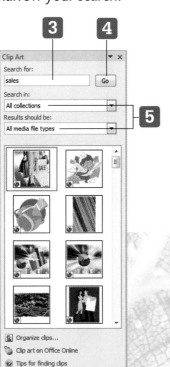

**? DID YOU KNOW?**
If you click Organize clips at the bottom of the Clip Art task pane, you open a browser that lets you view all the clip art collections by name and type.

**🔥 HOT TIP:** If a Microsoft Clip Organizer dialogue box appears when you click Go, click Yes to extend your search to the clip art Microsoft makes available to you online. If you're not online or want to keep your search options minimal, click No.

# Browse clip art online

If you don't find what you want in Office's built-in clip art collections, you can search additional clip art that Microsoft makes available to Office users on its website. You can also search for clip art available on other websites.

**1** Click Insert.

**2** Click Clip Art.

**3** Click Clip art on Office Online in the Clip Art dialogue box.

**4** When the Microsoft Office Online clip art page appears, enter a term in the Clip Art search box.

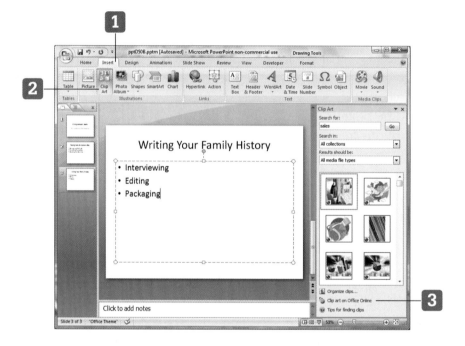

5 Click Search.

6 Tick the box of the image you want to add it to the 'Selection Basket'.

7 Click the magnifying glass next to the tick box to view more information about the image.

8 Click the Download link to save selected files to your computer.

**HOT TIP:** You can access the Microsoft Online clip art Web page directly at: http://office.microsoft.com/en-us/clipart/default.aspx

**ALERT:** Clip art isn't always free. You can freely use the art that Microsoft makes available to Office users, but artists who make their work available online sometimes charge a fee or require you to give them credit. Read the fine print before you use such images.

# Insert clip art

Once you locate an image from the Office clip art collections in the Clip Art task pane, you have several options for handling it. When you pass your mouse pointer over the thumbnail version of the image, a down arrow appears. Click it and you view a context menu that lets you perform various functions.

**1** Click Insert.

**2** Click the Clip Art button.

**3** Enter a keyword in the Search for box in the Clip Art task pane and click Go.

**4** Pass your mouse arrow over an image. Notice that an information box appears with details about the image file.

**5** Click the down arrow at the side of the image.

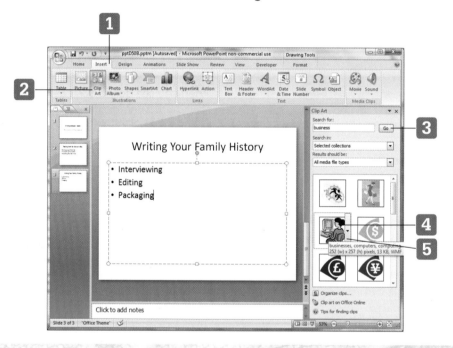

**6** Choose an option from the dropdown menu list:

- Insert to place the image in your document

- Copy to copy the image file to the Clipboard so that you can paste it elsewhere

- Delete from Clip Organizer to remove the image from the Office clip art collection

- Copy to Collection to copy the image to a collection

- Move to Collection to move the image from one collection to another

- Edit Keywords to add or delete keywords that describe the image

- Find Similar Style to find a similar image

- Preview/Properties to get a preview of the image and learn about its properties.

? **DID YOU KNOW?**

When you see details such as 254 (w) × 232 (h) pixels, it means that the image is 254 pixels wide by 232 pixels in height.

**WHAT DOES THIS MEAN?**

**Pixel:** A tiny rectangle that contains a bit of digital information. A digital image contains thousands or even millions of pixels.

**WMF:** Stands for Windows media file.

 **HOT TIP:** You can simply single-click the image itself to insert it in your document.

# Place a picture

Whether you have chosen an image from Office's clip art libraries or a photo taken with your digital camera, you can easily add it to a document. You can add a file from a CD-ROM, directly from your digital camera, from a Flash USB drive or from a file on your hard disk. Before you add the image, you can view a thumbnail to make sure it's the one you want.

1 Click the Insert tab.

2 Click Picture.

3 Click one of your Favorite links or the dropdown list arrow to locate an image.

4 Click an image file.

5 Click Insert.

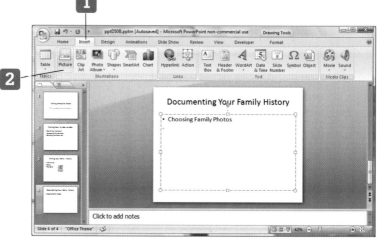

**? DID YOU KNOW?**

You can link to a file as well as insert it by clicking the dropdown list arrow next to Insert in the dialogue box and choosing Link to File.

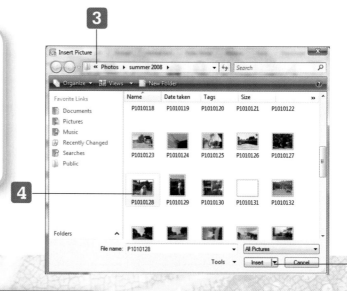

**HOT TIP:** Click the Photo Album button on the Insert tab to insert a series of images all at once.

# Adjust picture size

When you first add an image to a document, chances are it's too big for the available space. You have two options for resizing the image. You can click and drag the sizing handles on the sides of the frame that contains the image, or the corners, but be careful to resize it proportionately if you use the ones on the sides or you'll distort its appearance.

**1** Click the image to display the sizing handles on the sides and at the corners.

**2** Drag one of the side handles if you want to make the image narrower or shorter.

**3** Drag one of the corner handles to resize the object proportionately.

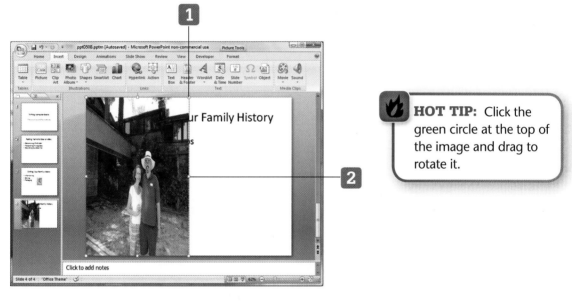

**HOT TIP:** Click the green circle at the top of the image and drag to rotate it.

**ALERT:** Be sure to press Ctrl + Z or click the Undo button if you change an image's size, then change your mind and want to revert to how it was before.

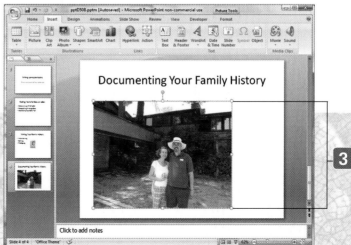

# Specify image size

Sometimes, you have a precise amount of space available to accommodate an image and you need to be able to specify the size with precision. If you need to make an image an exact width or height, you can enter the size manually using the Format menu's controls.

**1** Click the image to change the size.

**2** Click the Format tab under Picture Tools.

**3** Use the up or down arrows or type a size in the height and/or width dialogue boxes to specify the image size.

**4** Click the Size dialogue box launcher to choose Lock aspect ratio or change other options.

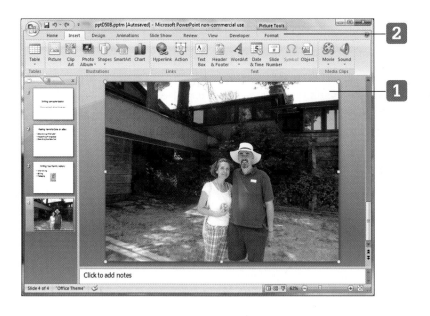

**? DID YOU KNOW?**

Picture Tools is one of the Ribbon tabs that appears only when you perform a certain function: when you select a table, or select an image, for instance.

# Add a border to a picture

If you are inserting a picture that needs to be demarcated from the surrounding text, a border can help. A border both separates text and images and calls attention to the image. The Picture Border button makes this easy, and allows you to change the border thickness and colour to complement the rest of your document's design.

**1** Click the image to display the selection handles around it.

**2** Click the Format tab under Picture Tools.

**3** Click the Picture Border button in the list of options below Format.

**4** Make selections from the dropdown menu that appears:

- Choose a colour to apply it to the border
- Choose More Outline Colors for more colour options
- Choose No Outline to delete the border
- Choose Weight and then choose an option from the submenu to assign a weight (or thickness) to the border
- Choose Dashes and then click an option on the submenu to make the border dashed rather than solid.

**HOT TIP:** Choose More Lines from the Dashes submenu if you don't see the line style you want in the initial selection.

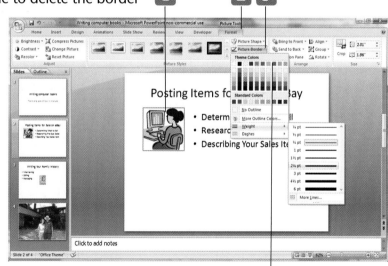

**DID YOU KNOW?**

If you don't see the colour you want in the dropdown menu or if you want to specify a colour by tying the R (Red), G (Green) and B (Blue) values, choose More Outline Colors from the submenu.

# Brighten up an image

Most photos that you take with a digital camera could benefit from some simple editing before you publish them online or in print. One of the simplest and most effective 'fixes' is to change the brightness of the image. By doing so you make the details of the image easier to view, especially if you plan to publish on the Web.

**1** Click the image to display the selection handles.

**2** Click the Format tab under Picture Tools.

**3** Click Brightness.

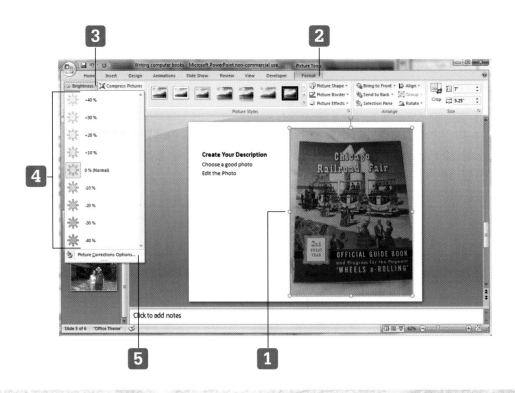

**4** Choose one of the following from the task pane:

- A negative value to make the image darker than it already is

- A positive value to make the image lighter.

**5** If you want more control over the brightness, choose Picture Corrections Options at the bottom of the task pane.

**6** Move the slider for brightness left or right to change the brightness one percentage point at a time, then click Close when you're happy.

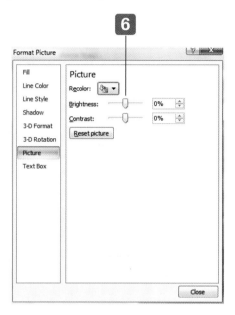

**DID YOU KNOW?**

If you are unhappy with your changes, just click Reset Picture to return it to its original appearance.

# Modify a picture's contrast

'Contrast' is the difference between the dark and light areas in an image. Contrast is most often seen in photographic images. In black-and-white images, for instance, the light and dark areas are broken into shades of grey. By increasing the contrast, you highlight the difference between the light and dark shades and the image looks more vivid and dramatic. By lowering contrast you make the image softer.

**1** Click the picture to display the selection handles as well as the Picture Tools ribbon.

**2** Click the Format tab under Picture Tools.

**3** Click Contrast.

**4** Choose one of the following from the task pane:

- A positive number to increase the contrast
- A negative number to decrease the contrast.

**5** Click Picture Corrections Options at the bottom of the task pane to access the contrast slider and change contrast one percentage point at a time.

Low contrast

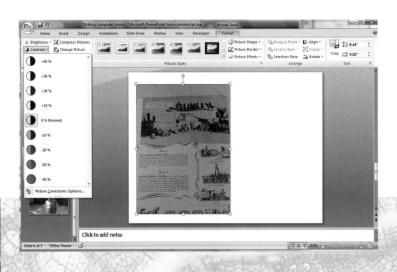

High contrast

# Change an image's colour scheme

The Format picture dialogue box that Office makes available has some surprisingly powerful features. One of those features is the ability to change the colour scheme of an image. You can change an image that is predominantly red to one that is blue, for instance, and adjust the brightness as you do so.

**1** Click the image to select it.

**2** Click Format.

**3** Click Recolor.

**4** Pass your mouse over each of the options given in the task pane to see the colour and brightness changes interactively. Click an option to select it.

**5** Click the More Variations option at the bottom of the task pane to choose a colour from a palette.

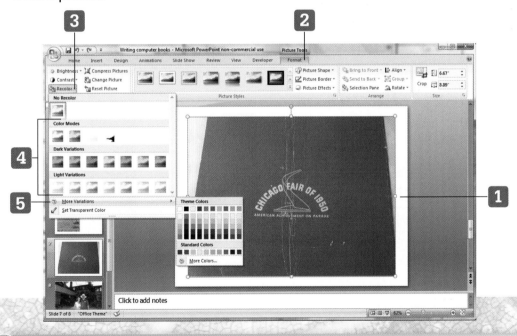

**?  DID YOU KNOW?**

Some image formats (Graphics Interchange Format – GIF – and Portable Network Graphics – PNG) have the ability to designate a colour as transparent. If you designate the colour that appears in the background of the image, the contents appear to be floating atop a transparent background.

# Crop and rotate a picture

Cropping is one of the most useful and effective options for editing a picture and preparing it for publication. Cropping not only focuses attention on the most important areas within an image but also makes the image physically smaller so it fits better on a page. It also makes the file size smaller.

**1** Click the image to select it.

**2** Click Format.

**3** Click Crop.

**4** Click and drag the side markers to make the image narrower or shorter.

**5** Click and drag the corner markers to delete the contents you want to crop out.

**6** Click anywhere outside the image when you've finished.

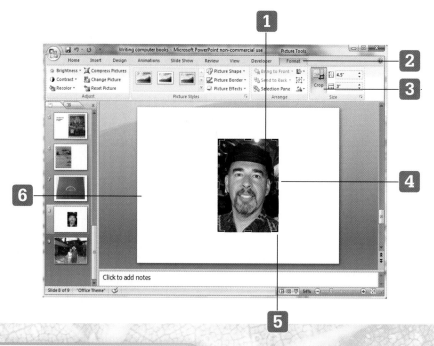

**? DID YOU KNOW?**

The areas you crop out haven't disappeared completely. Drag the markers outwards to restore them if you decide that you want to crop the image less tightly.

# Rotate an image

Sometimes, the contents of a photographic image aren't precisely vertical or horizontal. Equally, if you are inserting a piece of line art, you frequently want to rotate it so the contents point one way rather than another. In either case, you can improve the image and the way it relates to the rest of the page by rotating it.

**1** Select the image.

**2** Hover the mouse pointer over the green rotate button at the centre of the top of the object and drag to rotate it.

**3** Click anywhere outside the object to save the rotation.

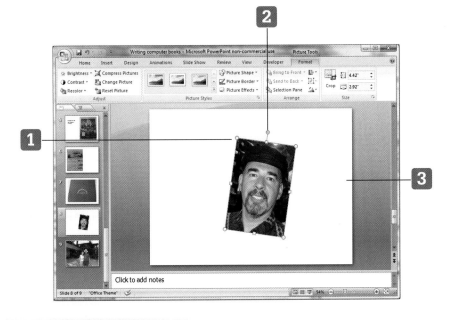

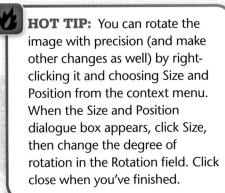

**HOT TIP:** You can rotate the image with precision (and make other changes as well) by right-clicking it and choosing Size and Position from the context menu. When the Size and Position dialogue box appears, click Size, then change the degree of rotation in the Rotation field. Click close when you've finished.

# Create WordArt text

WordArt is an Office feature that lets you create text-based graphics. It turns your text into colourful art that you can slant, turn into 3D or curve to follow a line. It's a great way to highlight an important message or make a page more interesting when you don't have photos or drawings to work with.

**1** Click the Insert tab.

**2** Click the WordArt button and choose a text style from the dropdown menu. A text box appears in the document with placeholder text that you can replace by typing your own text.

**3** Type the text you want to turn into WordArt.

**4** If you wish, use the font commands on the Home tab to change the appearance of your text.

**5** Position the text cursor in the WordArt text box if you want to edit the text.

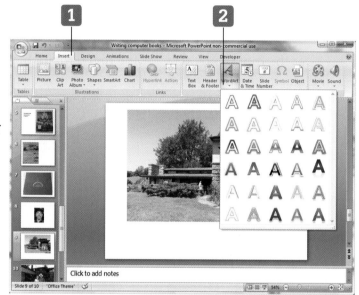

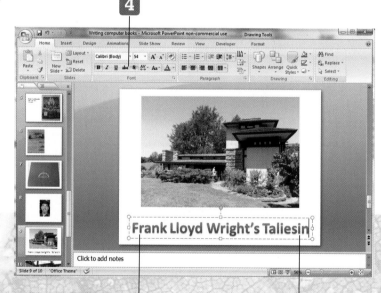

**ALERT:** Use WordArt sparingly – too much large-scale, brightly coloured and textured text can distract from the rest of a publication.

# Format WordArt

Once you have created some WordArt, you should explore the many options for spicing up its appearance. These options allow you to choose new styles, change the way the characters are filled and the outline styles around the characters.

**1** To change the current WordArt style, click the WordArt text to select it.

**2** Click the Format tab under Drawing Tools or WordArt Tools.

**3** Click the scroll arrows to browse through additional WordArt styles.

**4** Hover your mouse pointer over a style to view an interactive preview in your own text block. Click the style to select it.

**5** To change the fill, click the Text Fill or Shape Fill button and choose a colour, gradient or texture option.

**6** Click Text Outline or Shape Outline and choose a weight or dash style to change your WordArt outline style.

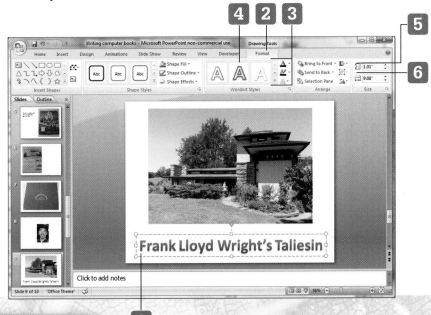

**? DID YOU KNOW?**

If you ever need to remove WordArt text, select it, click the Format tab, click the Quick Styles button, then click Clear WordArt.

# Apply special effects to WordArt

One of the best features of WordArt is that you can apply a range of special effects with just a few mouse clicks, without having to do any fancy drawing. The available effects include shadows, reflections, glow, 3D rotations and transformations.

**1** Click the WordArt text that you want to edit.

**2** Click Format under the Drawing Tools tab.

**3** Click the Text Effects button.

**4** Point to one of the Text Effects options, each of which has a different submenu of options:

- Shadow lets you choose to add shadows that give the characters a 3D effect

- Reflection adds a faint reflected image under each character

- Glow adds glow lines around the characters

- Bevel makes the characters appear to be lifted off the screen, as if carved out

- 3-D Rotation makes the images seem slanted and put in perspective

- Transform lets you draw characters along a path or make them appear warped.

**? DID YOU KNOW?**

You can always remove a style that you have applied using WordArt by selecting the WordArt text, pointing to the style in the Text Effects gallery and selecting the No effect option.

# Create SmartArt graphics

SmartArt graphics are images that illustrate processes or relationships between elements within an Office document. A SmartArt graphic can illustrate a list, a series of steps in a process, a cycle, a hierarchy of items or a pyramid. If you ever want to graphically depict this sort of content, you only need to select a SmartArt object, then create the text to go along with it.

**1** Click Insert.

**2** Click the SmartArt button.

**3** Choose the general type of SmartArt graphic you want from the list on the left of the task pane that pops up.

**4** Click the specific style you want from the centre of the box.

**5** Click OK to add the graphic to your document.

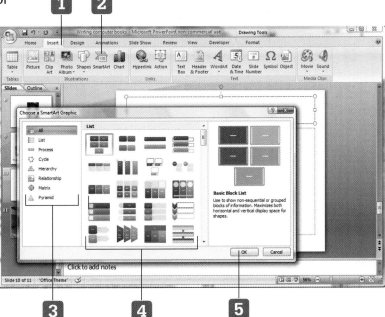

**HOT TIP:** If you are working with PowerPoint, right-click the content placeholder and choose Convert to SmartArt from the context menu.

**DID YOU KNOW?**
Your SmartArt graphic does not have to contain text – it can be an abstract design without labels. Simply insert the graphic and delete the placeholder text to leave it blank.

# Draw and resize shapes

Office may not include a drawing application as such, but it still gives you the ability to create shapes ready made for you. You can resize, edit, colour and fill the shapes freely to complement the rest of your document.

**1** Click Insert.

**2** Click the Shapes button.

**3** Click the shape you want to draw from the selections that pop up.

**4** Click at the place in the file where you want to add the shape, then drag to draw it.

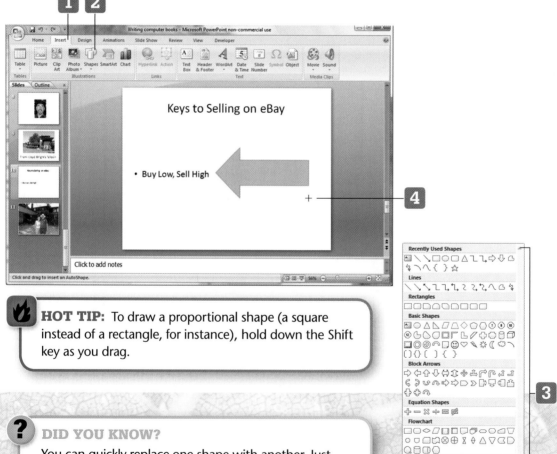

**HOT TIP:** To draw a proportional shape (a square instead of a rectangle, for instance), hold down the Shift key as you drag.

**DID YOU KNOW?**

You can quickly replace one shape with another. Just select the shape you have drawn, click Shapes, then choose another shape from the dropdown menu.

# Align and distribute objects

Once you have drawn multiple shapes or inserted a set of graphics, you can arrange them using Office's alignment tools. You have the option of making two or more objects snap to a grid or spacing two or more objects evenly. You can also align objects with a dividing line or other object.

**1** Select the objects you want to arrange.

**2** Click the Format tab under Drawing Tools.

**3** Click the Align button.

**4** Choose an alignment option from the dropdown menu that appears.

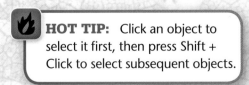

**HOT TIP:** Click an object to select it first, then press Shift + Click to select subsequent objects.

# Manage your images

An Office tool called Picture Manager allows you to manage, edit and share your images. It gives you a single interface for locating your images. Once you open your files, you can use Picture Manager to crop, rotate or otherwise edit an image.

**1** Click Start.

**2** Point to All Programs, click Microsoft Office, click Microsoft Office Tools, then Microsoft Office Picture Manager. When you first open Picture Manager, you are prompted to locate pictures on your computer.

**3** Click Locate pictures. Choose your disk drive from the dropdown list, then click OK.

**4** Click one of the View buttons to choose the way you want to view your images.

**5** Click an image and then choose Edit Pictures if you want to change it.

**6** When you've finished, click Close.

**? DID YOU KNOW?**

The Edit Pictures task pane, which opens when you click the Edit Pictures button, lets you remove red eye from an image. You can also resize an image or even compress a picture so that it takes up less disk space.

# 4 Applying themes and formatting

# Introduction

Office 2007 gives you a variety of ways to format documents to make them look professional and businesslike. The first level of formatting is represented by the text commands that are common to all Office applications – bold, italic, underline and heading styles, plus choices of typeface.

Once you get beyond the obvious formatting options, you discover that Office includes some very sophisticated tools for making documents look professionally designed. For instance, you can apply a design *theme* to your page. A theme is a coordinated set of colours and design elements that gives a document a particular look and feel. Office also gives you tools for formatting specialised content, such as tables, numbers in worksheets and comments you add to documents. All of these approaches are intended to make your words and data easier to interpret.

# Apply a theme to an existing document

Office makes two kinds of design themes available to you: predesigned themes that come ready to use and customised themes that you can create yourself. Each theme contains a palette of 12 complementary colours as well as preselected fonts and other special effects. You don't see the colours all at once – some are accent colours, used for elements such as drop shadows or hyperlinks. You can view and change any of the colours if you want to match certain colours that you use in your other publications.

1 Open the file to which you want to apply a theme.

2 Click either the Page Layout or Design tab.

3 Click the Themes or All Themes button to display the gallery of available themes.

4 Click the theme you want (or click Browse for Themes for more options) and that theme's fonts and colours will be applied to the current document.

**ALERT:** If you are using Word, your document must be saved in Word 2007 format rather than as a Word 97-2003 (Compatibility Mode) document in order to use themes.

**? DID YOU KNOW?**

When you pass your mouse arrow over a theme, the colours appear in a live preview in the document that is currently open.

# Apply a theme to a new document

You can also apply a theme as part of the process of creating a new Office document. Themes are incorporated into each of the standard documents that come with Office as templates (fax cover sheets, letters, resumes, and so on). When you do choose a template, the background, text, graphics, charts and tables are automatically coordinated to the theme's look and feel. You only have to replace the placeholder text with your own content. You can always change the theme by choosing an option from the Themes submenu.

**1** Click the Office button.

**2** Click New.

**3** Click Installed Templates.

**4** Choose the template you want from the options that appear. Each template has a theme name assigned to it: Equity, Urban and so on.

**5** Click Create.

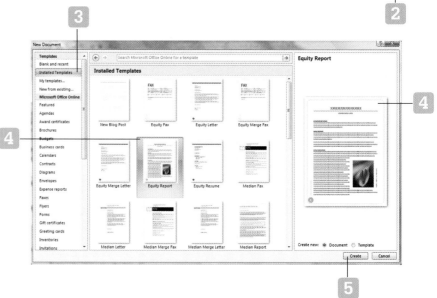

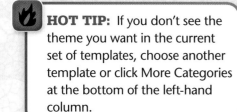

**HOT TIP:** If you don't see the theme you want in the current set of templates, choose another template or click More Categories at the bottom of the left-hand column.

**? DID YOU KNOW?**

You aren't limited to the themes that come with Office 2007 – you can also search for themes at Microsoft Office Online. Click the Themes button, then click Search Themes at Microsoft Office Online. Follow the instructions on the website to download and apply Office themes.

# Apply a theme from another document

If you have created a custom theme or have a theme that you want to use in multiple files, for consistency, you can quickly take the desired theme's attributes and apply them to a new document.

**1** Open the document to which you want to apply the theme.

**2** Click the Design or Page Layout tab.

**3** Click Themes.

**4** Click Browse for Themes.

**5** Locate and select the Office document that contains the theme you want to use.

**6** Click Apply.

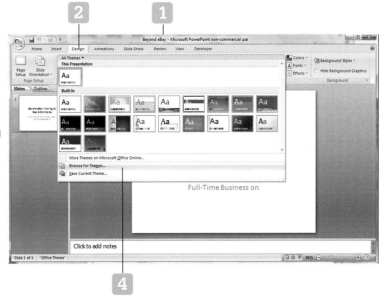

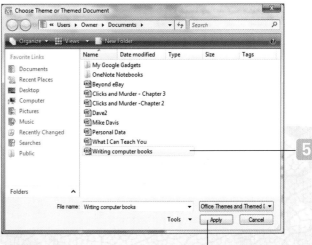

**?** **DID YOU KNOW?**

If you use Outlook, the Themes button is to be found on the Options tab.

# Change the default Office theme

Every Office document you create has a theme applied to it, whether you specifically select a theme or not. By default, the Office theme is applied to it, even if the file is completely blank. The Office theme has a white background, black text and other subtle colours, such as blue for hyperlinks. If you get tired of the generic Office theme or want to consistently apply themes to all of your files, you can change it.

In Excel and Word, you need to create a new, default workbook or worksheet template.

## In Word

**1** Press Ctrl + N to create a new blank document.

**2** On the Home tab, click Change Styles, point to Style Set, then choose the design you want to use.

**3** Click Change Styles again, point to Colors, then choose the colours you want.

**4** Click Change Styles, point to Fonts, then choose the fonts you want.

**5** Click Change Styles and choose Set as Default.

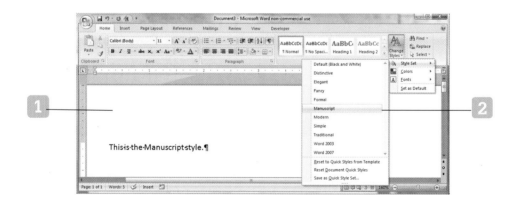

**DID YOU KNOW?**

In PowerPoint, on the Design tab, right-click the theme you want and choose Set as Default Theme from the context menu.

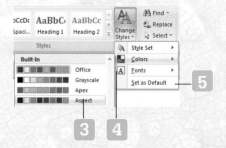

## In Excel

1. Press Ctrl + N to open a new blank workbook.

2. Click the Page Layout tab.

3. Click Themes.

4. Select the theme you want.

5. Click the Office button, point to Save As and choose Excel Workbook.

6. Choose Excel Template from the Save as type dropdown list and click Save.

**? DID YOU KNOW?**

If you want to save a workbook with the default theme, name it sheet.xltx instead of book.xltx.

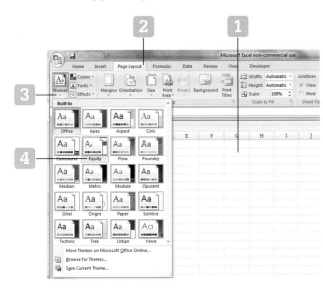

**? DID YOU KNOW?**

You can also create a default theme from an existing workbook that has the theme you want. Click the Office button, click New, click New from existing, then locate the workbook you want to use. Click the workbook, click Create New, click Themes and choose the themes you want. Then follow the steps given in this task.

# Change theme colours

Each of Office's themes comes with a set of coordinated colours, but you can incorporate your own colour scheme into a theme. It's a great option for anyone who is interested in graphic design and familiar with red, green, blue (RGB) and other colour modes. Once you have added colours to a theme, you can add it to Office's collection of colour themes so that it's available for any document.

1 Open the file to which you want to add new colours.

2 Click the Page Layout or Design tab.

3 Click Theme Colors.

4 If you want to apply a theme's colours to the current document, choose a set of colours from the dropdown list.

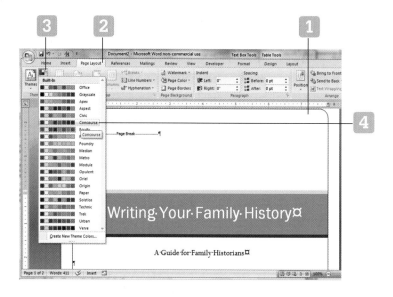

# Create your own theme colours

If you don't see the colours you want on the dropdown menu that appears when you click Theme Colors, you can create your own.

Follow Steps 1 to 4 given in the preceding task, then do the following:

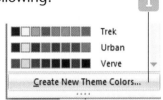

1. Choose Create New Theme Colors, at the bottom of the list of theme colours.

2. Click the buttons for the colours you want to add – if you want to create your own Text/Background colour, click that, for instance.

3. Either choose a standard colour from the palette that appears or choose More Colors…

4. Click a new colour from the Standard or Custom tab, and click OK.

5. Type a new name for your colour.

6. Click Save.

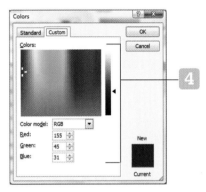

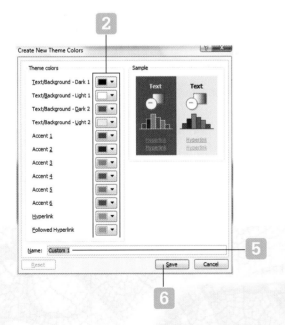

## DID YOU KNOW?

If you ever want to edit your customised colour theme, click the Page Layout tab, click Theme Colors, right-click the colour you want to edit, click Edit, click Delete, then click Yes.

# Change theme fonts

Each Office theme has a set of fonts chosen for it. You can change the fonts just as easily as you can change the colours.

1  Open the document with the theme fonts that you want to change.

2  Click the Page Layout or Design tab.

3  Click the Theme Fonts button.

4  Pass your mouse over the fonts shown to view previews of those fonts in the open document.

5  Click a font to add it to the theme.

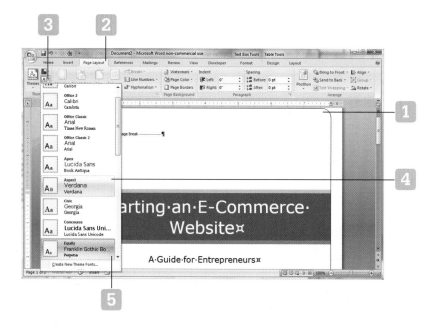

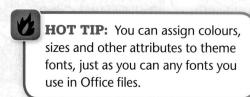

**HOT TIP:** You can assign colours, sizes and other attributes to theme fonts, just as you can any fonts you use in Office files.

# Add special effects to themes

Themes include not only fonts and colours but also special effects. These effects include lines, charts, files and other elements that give flavour to your theme. Whether you're editing an existing theme or creating your own custom one, be sure to pay attention to these additional features.

1 Open the document that you want to add the effects to.

2 Click the Page Layout or Design tab.

3 Click the Themes' Effects button.

4 Click the set of theme effects you want from the dropdown menu.

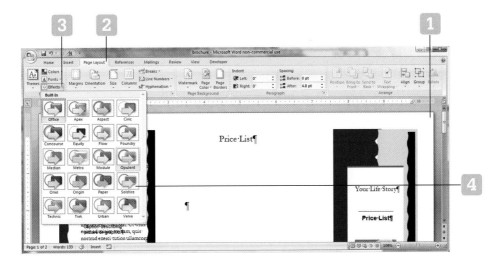

**DID YOU KNOW?**

The theme effects your document is using currently appear highlighted in the dropdown menu.

# Create a custom theme

If you want to be able to exercise the ultimate level of control over your Office files, consider creating a theme. By creating a theme rather than designing the file from scratch, you gain the ability to quickly apply the theme elements from one file to another. This is ideal for an office environment, where coworkers need to create publications that have a consistent look and feel.

1 Press Ctrl + N to open a new blank file.

2 Click the Page Layout or Design tab.

3 By Themes, Fonts click the Colors and Effects buttons and choose the elements you want your theme to have.

4 Click the Themes button and choose Save Current Theme.

5 Type a name for the theme you are creating.

6 Click Save.

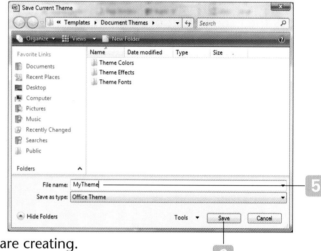

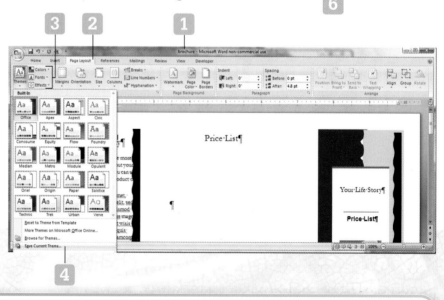

 **DID YOU KNOW?**

If you ever want to remove a customised theme from the menu of themes, move or delete the file. Themes are located in the Document Themes folder within the Office folder.

# Rotate and flip objects

The exercises up to this point have examined design themes, which affect a whole file, but you can also format just specific design elements, such as images, that you insert in a file.

One quick and dramatic way in which you can format an image or other object is to flip or rotate it. Office applications give you controls for performing these functions. If you flip an object, you turn it 180 degrees in the opposite direction. Rotating turns the object 90 degrees to the right or left. You also have the option to freely rotate an object.

1. Select the object you want to flip or rotate.

2. Click the Format tab.

3. Click Rotate in the Arrange group of buttons.

4. Choose one of the rotation options that appear in order to rotate the object 90 degrees to the right or left.

5. Choose a flip option to flip the object.

6. Click and drag one of the green free rotation dots round the object to rotate it freely.

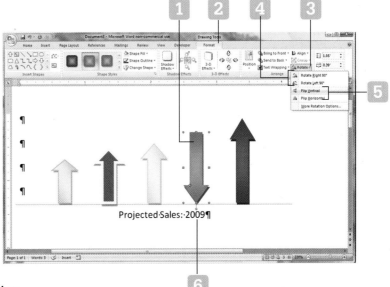

 **DID YOU KNOW?**

If you choose the More Rotation Options from the bottom of the Rotate dropdown list, you can specify a definite number of degrees through which the object will move.

# Make an object 3D

Usually, artists have to employ some drawing ability to add the accents that give an object a three-dimensional appearance, but when you select an object in Office, whether it is three-dimensional or not, you can turn to the 3D controls on the Format tab and add such special effects even if you have no such ability.

**1** Click the Insert tab, then Shapes.

**2** Draw a simple two-dimensional shape, such as a rectangle, and leave the image selected.

**3** On the Format tab, click 3-D Effects.

**4** Choose 3-D Effects.

**5** Pass your mouse pointer over an option to view the effect.

**6** Click a 3D option to select it.

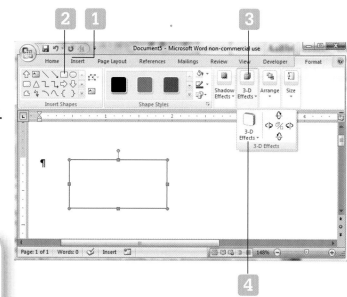

**? DID YOU KNOW?**

The four options next to the 3-D Effects button on the 3-D Effects dropdown list let you quickly add shadowing to an object and rotate it to the left or right.

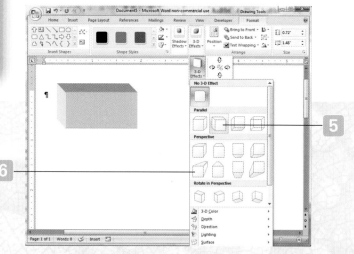

# Change stacking order

Suppose you have multiple images in a file and you want the images to overlap for a compact and sophisticated effect. You can change the 'stacking order' of those objects so that one appears atop the other ones.

1 Select the objects that you want to stack differently.

2 Click the Format tab.

3 Click the Bring to Front or Send to Back options and choose one of the following from the dropdown list commands:

- Bring to Front brings the item to the top of the stack
- Bring Forward brings the item up one position in the stack
- Send to Back sends the item to the bottom of the stack
- Send Backward sends the item one position down in the stack.

**? DID YOU KNOW?**

Bring to Front of Text or Send Behind Text only works if your document contains a mixture of text and graphics.

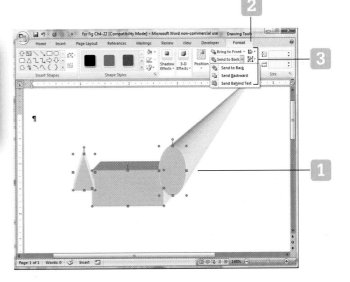

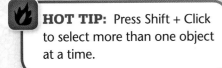
**HOT TIP:** Press Shift + Click to select more than one object at a time.

# Adjust shadows

Shadows don't make an object look three-dimensional, but they do add a sense of depth to the object. By throwing a shadow behind the object at a particular angle, the drawing looks far more professional than it would otherwise. Office's Format tab gives you a wide variety of shadow styles to choose from.

1 Select the object you want to format.

2 Click the Format tab.

3 Click the Shadow Effects button.

4 Click Shadow Effects in the box that pops up.

5 Choose an option from the dropdown menu that appears.

**? DID YOU KNOW?**

The object to which you add a shadow can be either two-dimensional or three-dimensional to begin with. If it was three-dimensional, the three-dimensional shaping will be replaced by shadowing.

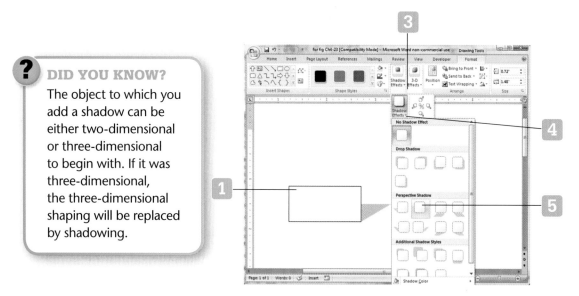

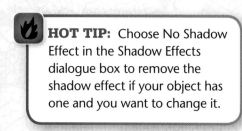

**HOT TIP:** Choose No Shadow Effect in the Shadow Effects dialogue box to remove the shadow effect if your object has one and you want to change it.

# Format text in tables

Tables give you a user-friendly way to present information in rows and columns. When you select a table or individual parts (rows, columns or cells), the Table Tools heading appears above the Ribbon. The Design and Layout tabs under Table Tools give you many commands for formatting tables in the way that you want.

1 Select the cells you want to format.

2 Click the Layout tab.

3 Click the Text Direction button to send text in the selected cells in a different direction.

4 Click one of the Alignment buttons to choose how text in the selected cells is aligned.

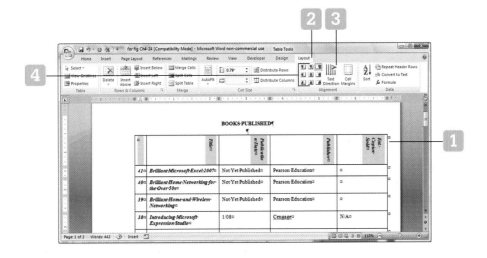

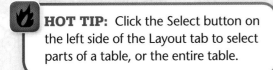

**HOT TIP:** Click the Select button on the left side of the Layout tab to select parts of a table, or the entire table.

**SEE ALSO:** In Chapter 5, you will learn how to create a table and begin working with data.

# Use Quick Styles to format a table

Office provides you with a set of predesigned table layouts that you can instantly apply. You will find them via the Design tab – just choose the one you want from the colourful gallery of options.

1 Click anywhere in the table you want to format.

2 Click the Design tab.

3 Click one of the scroll arrows to navigate through the Quick Styles options.

4 Click the style you want to apply it to the table.

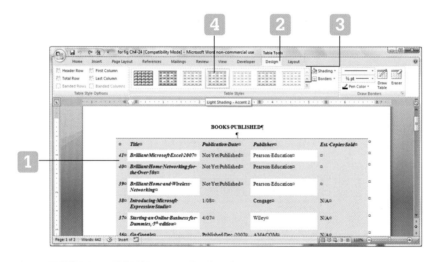

**HOT TIP:** When you reach the bottom of the list of table styles, click the More list arrow in the Table Styles group.

# Format numbers in worksheets

Office 2007 provides Excel users with a new feature – the Number Format dropdown list. Using this you can quickly format the appearance of numbers in cells. You are able to change the way the numbers look without changing the values themselves.

**1** Select the cell or range of cells you want to format.

**2** Click the Home tab if necessary.

**3** Click the Number Format dropdown list and choose one of the available formats:

- General – no formatting

- Number – 1.50

- Currency – £1.50

- Accounting – £98.00 rather than £98

- Short Date – 17/10/2009

- Long Date – Tuesday, 21 October, 2008

- Time – 3:30:00 PM

- Percentage – 33.33%

- Fraction – $\frac{1}{2}$

- Scientific – 3.50E ÷ 02.

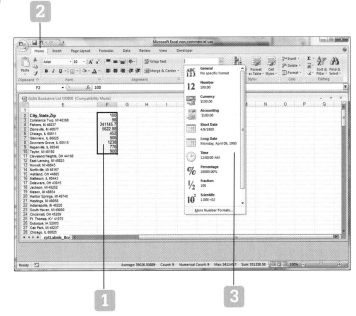

**? DID YOU KNOW?**

Just below the Number Format list, you will see a set of numbers that let you do specialised formatting: Currency Style, Percent Style, Comma Style, Increase Decimal, Decrease Decimal.

**? DID YOU KNOW?**

You can apply more than one type of formatting to the data you have selected.

# Use the Format Cells dialogue box

You can format numbers within cells the old-fashioned way, too. If you want a more familiar formatting interface than the new Number Format list provides, follow the steps below to use the Format Cells dialogue box.

1 Select the cell or range of cells that you want to format.

2 Click the Home tab if necessary.

3 Click the Number dialogue box launcher.

The Format Cells dialogue box opens with the Number tab in front.

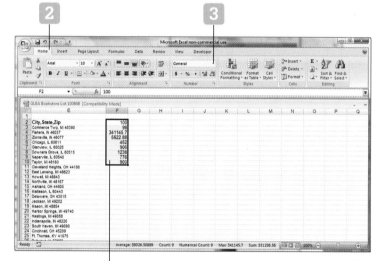

4 Select the options that you want.

5 Preview your selection in the Sample box.

6 Click OK.

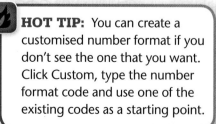

**HOT TIP:** You can create a customised number format if you don't see the one that you want. Click Custom, type the number format code and use one of the existing codes as a starting point.

# Work with the Format Painter

The Format Painter is easy to overlook, but once you learn to use it, it can save you lots of time choosing formatting options from the Ribbon. The Format Painter lets you copy all of the formatting attributes from one element to another. If you have formatted one paragraph in 14 pt Helvetica bold italic type using small caps, when you type another paragraph and you have not done this formatting already, it can be time-consuming to choose all of those options. The Format Painter lets you paint them on to the new paragraph.

1 Select the cell, range or text that contains the formatting attributes that you want to copy.

2 Click the Home tab if necessary.

3 Click the Format Painter button below Home.

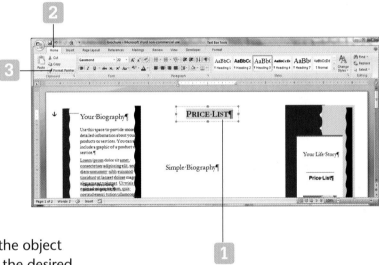

4 Select the text or click the object that you want to apply the desired formatting to. That formatting is applied.

5 If you double-clicked the Format Painter, apply the formatting to other objects as needed. Press Esc when you've finished.

**? DID YOU KNOW?**
The cursor turns into a paintbrush icon when the Format Painter has been selected.

**HOT TIP:** If you plan to copy the formatting to more than one element, double-click the Format Painter.

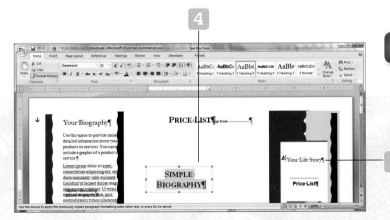

# 5 Creating a Word document

# Introduction

Microsoft Office Word 2007 gives you all the tools and features you'll need to create business, personal and other documents that convey your message and make you look good in the process. Word 2007 is more sophisticated than preceding versions. It contains auto recovery features that reduce the chances of you losing information if your system crashes or you encounter another computer problem.

Word 2007 is also ideal for working in a collaborative environment. It gives you the ability to track changes to files and record those changes in comments that are easy for others to read. You can also compare separate versions of the same file to see what changes have been made.

Word has been specially designed to work with text, but it has formatting features that go well beyond simple word processing of documents. Word files are based on templates that contain predesigned fonts, colours and margins, among other features. You can modify the template styles to meet your publishing needs and create professional documents, such as newsletters, invitations, posters and other eye-catching presentations.

# Change document views

Word provides you with different ways to view a file so that you can work with its content more easily. Each view corresponds to what you might need to do with the file – that is, Print Layout shows you how each page is laid out when printed, Full Screen Reading shows you the maximum amount of text all at once, Web Layout shows you how the file will look online, Outline shows you the contents arranged as an outline and Draft shows you the file as a single long document without top or bottom margins (page breaks are indicated by a single dashed line).

**1** Click the View tab.

**2** Choose one of the five buttons in the Document Views group.

**3** Alternatively, click one of the view buttons on the status bar at the bottom of the screen. Pass your mouse pointer over each of the buttons and a little box will appear with words saying what each one does.

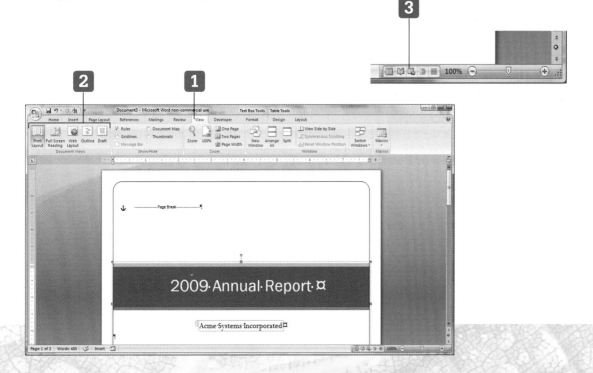

# Make text easier to read

If you are having trouble reading text because the characters are too small, you can change to Full Screen Reading, then try some other view options to make the words bigger.

**1** Click the View tab.

**2** Click Full Screen Reading.

**3** Click the View Options button.

**4** Click Increase Text Size on the dropdown menu.

**5** Click the Close button. You are returned to the document.

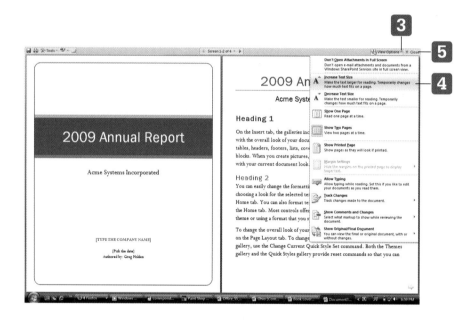

**HOT TIP:** Press the Esc key to move out of Full Screen Reading and return to Print Layout.

# View multiple pages

When you are in Full Screen Reading view, you gain access to the View Options menu, which gives you alternatives for viewing your content. Two particularly useful commands are the Show One Page and Show Two Pages options, which let you switch between these two views.

**1** While in Full Screen Reading view, click View Options.

**2** Choose Show One Page.

**3** Choose Show Two Pages to switch to viewing two pages side by side.

**4** When you've finished, click Close.

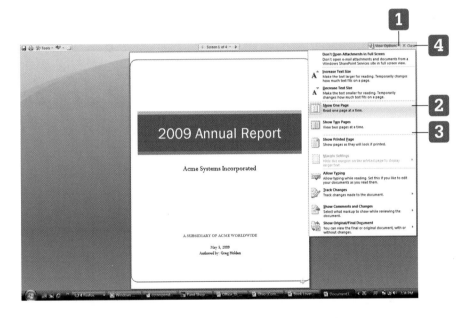

**? DID YOU KNOW?**

The View Options menu includes options to disable the opening of email attachments while you are in Full Screen Reading view. Other options include Show Printed Page, which lets you preview how the page will look before it prints; Margin Settings, which lets you hide the margins on the printed page to display larger text; Allow Typing, which allows you to type in the document while in Full Screen Reading view; Track Changes, which lets you view revisions you or others have made; Show Comments and Changes; and Show Original/Final Document, which lets you view either an original file (before changes) or the final version of the file (after changes).

# View a document map

A document map is an outline that displays headings and subsections within a file. Document Map view is available when you are in Full Screen Reading view. The map appears in a column on the left side of the screen, whether you are viewing one or two pages at a time.

**1** While you are in Full Screen Reading view, click the Navigation button, which appears at the centre of the top of the page.

**2** Click View Options.

**3** Choose Document Map.

**4** Click a link in the document map on the left to jump to that part of the file.

**5** When you've finished, click Close.

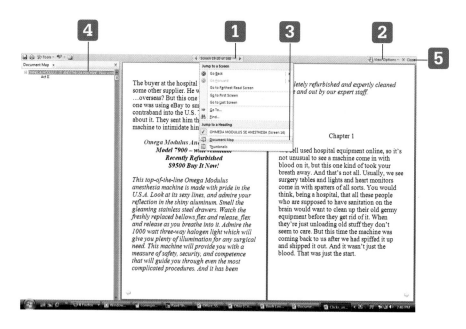

**? DID YOU KNOW?**

The Thumbnails option at the bottom of the list lets you view thumbnail images of each page in your file instead of a series of links on the left side of the page.

# Set up the page

Every document has a page setup – that is, a set of formatting instructions that describes how you view the contents and how they are printed. The page layout instructions that comprise page setup include its size (letter, legal, A4 or envelope) and its orientation (portrait or landscape). To set up a page's orientation, follow the steps given below.

**1** Click the Page Layout tab.

**2** Click Orientation below the tab.

**3** Choose Landscape or Portrait to set the orientation.

**4** Click Size to set the size.

 **DID YOU KNOW?**

The portrait orientation has the smaller sides at the top and the bottom – for instance, in Portrait the top is 21 cm while the sides are 27.9 cm. In Landscape orientation the measurements are reversed.

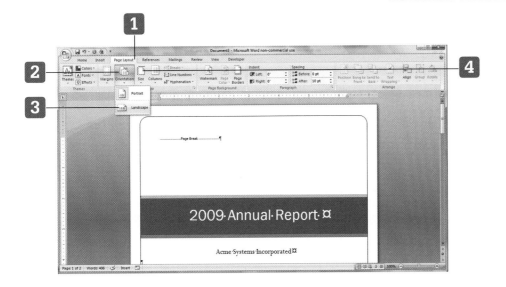

2009·Annual·Report·¤

Acme·Systems·Incorporated¤

# Set page margins visually

'Margins' are the blank areas around the four sides of a document. When you're working onscreen, margins help to make text more readable, but they are more valuable when you print a file. The 'gutter' is the space between left and right pages – the right margin of the left-hand (or even-numbered page) and the left margin of the right-hand (or odd-numbered) page. Office lets you change page margins visually using your mouse.

**1** Click the Ruler tickbox on the View tab if the ruler is not already displayed.

**2** Click the Page Layout tab.

**3** Hover your mouse pointer over a margin boundary on either the horizontal or vertical ruler.

**4** Press and hold Alt, then click a margin boundary to visually display the margin.

**5** Drag each of the margins (left, right, top, bottom) to change them as needed.

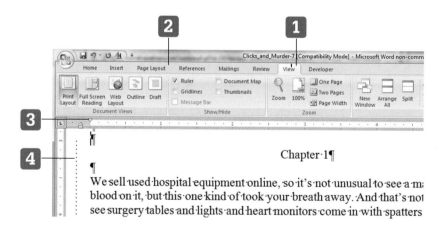

**?** **DID YOU KNOW?**

By default, Word documents have margins of 2.5 cm at the top and bottom, 3.2 cm on the left and right.

**?** **DID YOU KNOW?**

You can also use the Page Setup dialogue box to set up a page. Click the Page Layout tab, click Margins, then click Custom Margins to open the Page Setup dialogue box.

# Create an outline

An outline is a hierarchical way of organising a set of information into categories and subcategories. You can either create an outline from scratch while in Outline view or else convert the items in a bulleted or numbered list into an outline. The steps given below will get you started if you want to create an outline from scratch.

**1** Open a new file and click the Page Layout tab.

**2** Click the Outline View button.

**3** Type a heading for your outline, then press Enter.

**4** If you need to change the heading level to a higher or lower one, position the insertion point at the beginning of the heading and click the Promote or Demote buttons.

**5** Move to the next line and type a subheading or item in the outline. As before, click the Promote or Demote buttons to change the level as needed.

**6** When you've finished, click Close Outline View.

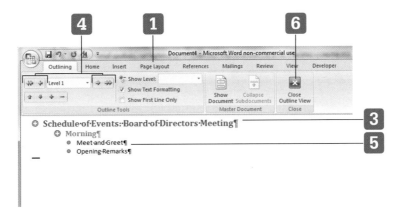

**? DID YOU KNOW?**

You can also position the cursor anywhere in a heading and click the Move Up or Move Down buttons until it is positioned correctly in the outline.

# Add a new page or section

Adding a new page is an essential part of document creation, but not all page breaks are the same.

When you add content and a new page is automatically added to accommodate it, that is a soft page break. When you manually insert a page break before the page is filled, you create a hard page break. You can also create a section break. A section is a separate document within a larger document. Each section can have its own page numbering, margins, page orientation and so on.

**1** Click to position the cursor at the point where you want to insert a hard page break.

**2** Do one of the following:

- To insert a page break, click Insert, then click the Page Break button.

- To insert a blank page, click Insert, then click the Blank Page button.

- To insert a section break, click the Page Layout button, click Page Break, then click the page break or section break option you want.

**3** If you need to delete a page break, click the page break to select it and press the Delete key.

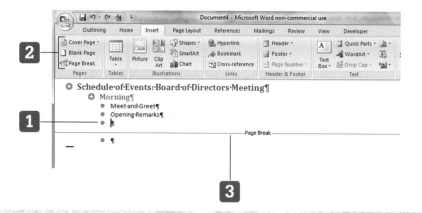

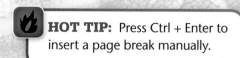

**HOT TIP:** Press Ctrl + Enter to insert a page break manually.

# Add headers and footers

A 'header' is content that appears in the top margin of a Word document page and a 'footer' is content that appears in the bottom. The most common content of a header or footer is a page number. Headers and footers also typically contain a date, an author's name, the title of the work or the title of an individual section.

Word 2007 also offers a new feature – predefined headers and footers that you can add with a single mouse click.

**1** Click the Insert tab.

**2** Click the Header or Footer button.

**3** Choose one of the preformatted headers or footers.

**4** Click Edit Footer at the bottom of the box if you need to modify one you have already edited.

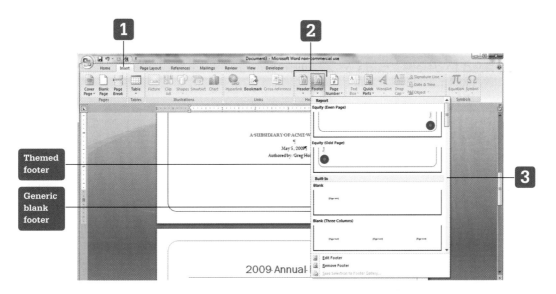

Themed footer

Generic blank footer

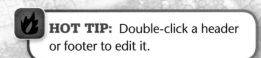

**HOT TIP:** Double-click a header or footer to edit it.

**5** Click the Design Tab, under Header & Footer Tools, to format the header or footer.

**6** When you've finished, click Close Header and Footer.

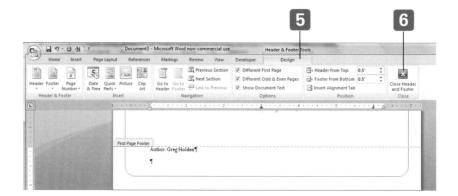

 **DID YOU KNOW?**

If your document uses one of the Office 2007 themes, the headers or footers you see when you click the Header or Footer button will have the same theme. A set of generic blank themes will also appear.

# Insert page numbers

There's no need to add page numbers manually (typing them yourself on each page). Office 2007 lets you add page numbers quickly and updates them automatically as your content changes. You can insert preformatted page numbers and ensure that your document uses different page number positioning on odd and even pages.

**1** Click the Insert tab.

**2** Click the Page Number button under Header & Footer Tools.

**3** Click one of the positioning options from the list that pops up and specific submenu designs.

**4** Click the Design tab under Header & Footer Tools to format the page number.

**5** Tick the boxes to change the formatting depending on the page number.

**6** When you've finished, click Close Header and Footer.

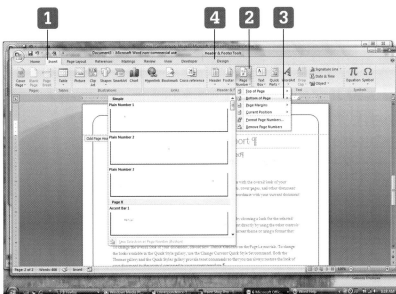

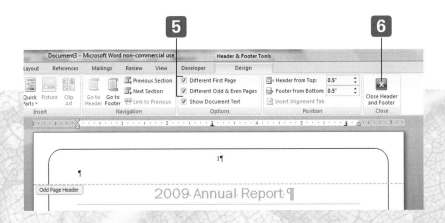

# Add the date and time

Office 2007 keeps track of the current date and time as recorded by your computer's internal calendar and clock. You are not only able to insert the current date and time but also can insert it in any installed language. Adding such a 'timestamp' makes it easier to track different versions of your file.

**1** Click the Insert tab.

**2** Click the text to position the cursor where you want the date and time to appear.

**3** Click the Design tab under Header & Footer Tools in the Insert group.

**4** Click the Date & Time button.

**5** Click the Language box, top right, and select the language if needed.

**6** Choose the desired format from those given on the left.

**7** Tick the Update automatically box to automatically update the date or time.

**8** Click OK.

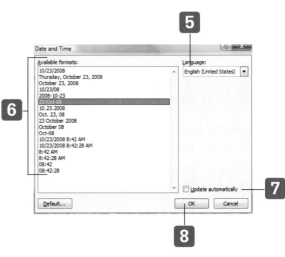

**ALERT:** Be sure to first display or insert a header or footer and position the cursor there before inserting the date and time.

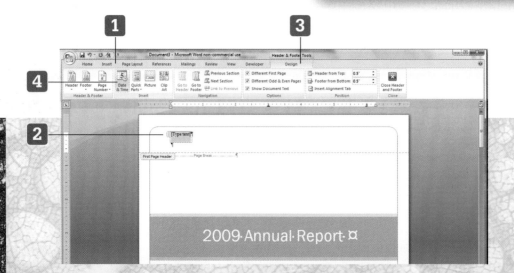

# Find and replace formatting

Word 2007's Find and Replace tool is powerful, allowing you to find text and other characters and limit your search to whole words. It also gives you a way to find elements that have particular formatting attributes.

**1** Click the Home tab if necessary.

**2** Click the Find button in the Editing group.

**3** Click No Formatting to clear any previous formatting choices.

**4** Click More at the bottom of the Find and Replace dialogue box, click Format and choose the formatting you want to find.

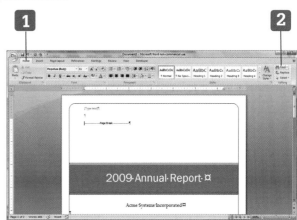

**5** Click Find Next to find the next instance of text with the formatting applied.

**6** Click OK and then click Close.

**?** **DID YOU KNOW?**

When you search for formatting, you don't necessarily have to search for specific text. You can also search for bookmarks, comments or other secondary elements in a Word file. Click the Home tab, click the down arrow next to Find, click the Go To tab, select the type of item you want to find, then click Next.

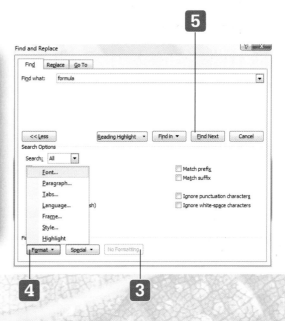

**SEE ALSO:** See Chapter 2 for the basic techniques for finding and replacing text.

# Set paragraph tabs

Tab stops in a Word file control how text or data aligns relative to the document margins. A tab stop defines where the content should align when you press the tab key. By default, tab stops are set at every 1.3 cm. You can set one of four tab stops: left, right, centre and decimal. The Tab button to the left of the horizontal ruler lets you switch between the different types of tabs.

1 Select one or more paragraphs that you want to align with the tab stop.

2 Click the Tab button repeatedly until you see the type of tab stop you want.

3 Click the ruler at the point where you want to insert the tab stop.

4 Drag the tab stop to the right or left to adjust its position.

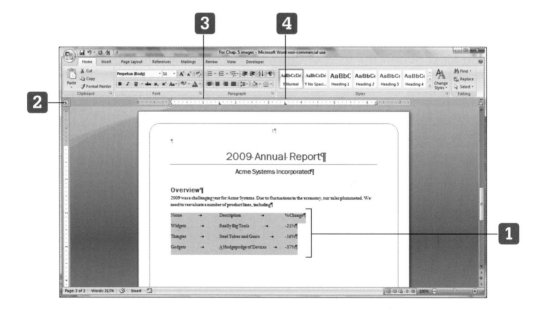
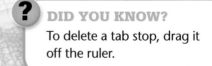
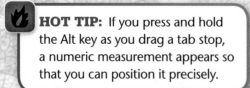

**HOT TIP:** If you press and hold the Alt key as you drag a tab stop, a numeric measurement appears so that you can position it precisely.

**DID YOU KNOW?**
To delete a tab stop, drag it off the ruler.

# Change character spacing

You can go weeks or months without thinking about adjusting the default character spacing – that is, the spacing between individual characters in text. You have two options: adjust the spacing between all characters in a uniform way using the Font dialogue box commands or change the kerning for individual characters. 'Kerning' is the print and design term for character spacing.

**1** Select the text you want to format.

**2** Click the Home tab if needed.

**3** Click the Font dialogue box launcher by clicking the little symbol at the bottom right of the Font group of buttons.

**4** Click the Character Spacing tab at the top of the box that appears.

**5** Click the Spacing dropdown list and choose an option (Expanded, for instance). Click the up or down arrows next to the By boxes to choose the amount of change.

**6** View the results in the preview area.

**7** Click OK when it's as you want it.

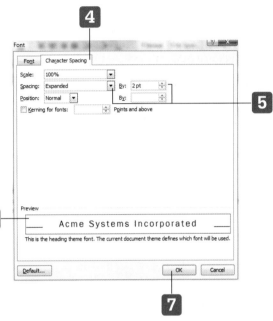

**? DID YOU KNOW?**

Tick the Kerning for fonts box to adjust the kerning for TrueType or Adobe Type Manager fonts.

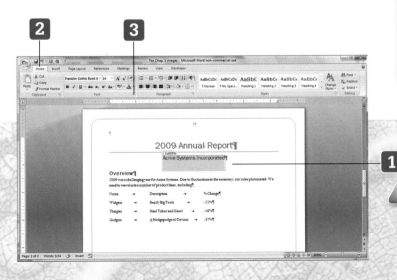

**! ALERT:** Kerning only works with TrueType or Adobe Type Manager fonts.

# Apply a style set

One of Word 2007's new features is the ability to add predefined style sets that help you format an entire document. Each style set has its own colours, fonts and other formatting combinations. The style sets have names that describe how they look: Classic, Elegant, Simple, Modern, Formal, Fancy and Distinctive.

1 Click the Home tab if necessary.

2 Click the Change Styles button in the Styles group.

3 Point to Style Set in the box that pops up and choose the style you want from the submenu that appears.

**? DID YOU KNOW?**

The Reset Document Quick Styles option beneath the list of style sets lets you reset the document to using Quick Styles again – the styles shown in the gallery in the Home Ribbon.

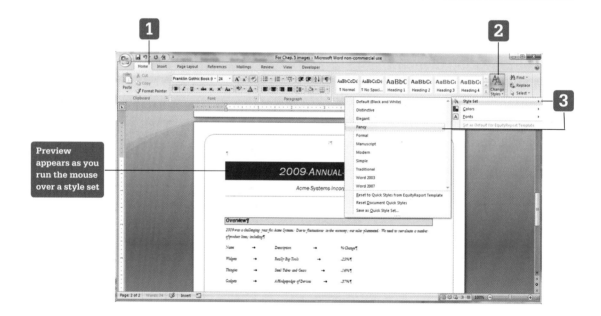

Preview appears as you run the mouse over a style set

# Create a style

Word 2007 comes with an extensive set of built-in styles, but if you need to create a style that's not included, you can do so easily. When you create a new style and save it with your own name, you can apply it quickly to paragraphs or characters in other files.

**1** Create text that has the formatting you want to save as a style and select that text.

**2** On the Home tab, Click the More arrow in the Styles group and choose Save Selection as a New Quick Style at the bottom of the box.

**3** Type a short and easy-to-remember name for your style in the Name box.

**4** Click Modify.

**5** Click Style type and choose either Paragraph or Character to denote the type of formatting that you want the style to have.

**6** Select any of the formatting options you want from the Formatting section.

**7** Tick the Add to Quick Style list box and click OK twice.

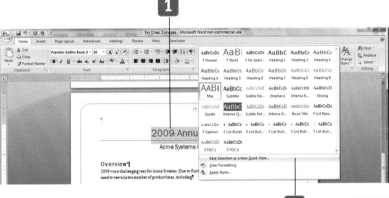

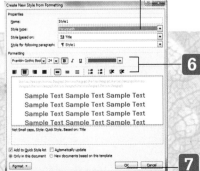

**?  DID YOU KNOW?**

There are two types of style. Paragraph formats all of the text within a paragraph, while Character is a group of formatting commands applied to any word, letter or block of text in a file.

# Modify a style

Whether you are working with a style of your own creation or else a Quick Style or style set that Word 2007 has provided, you can easily modify that style to suit your needs.

**1** On the Home tab, click the More list arrow in the Styles group.

**2** Right-click the name of the style you want to modify in the box, then choose Modify from the list in the box that pops up.

**3** Change the formatting attributes that you want to modify from the options in the Formatting section.

**4** Click Format, then choose the type of formatting you want to modify (font or paragraph).

**5** When you're happy, click OK.

**? DID YOU KNOW?**

If you want to add the new style to the Quick Style gallery, check that it isn't there already, then tick the Add to Quick Style list box.

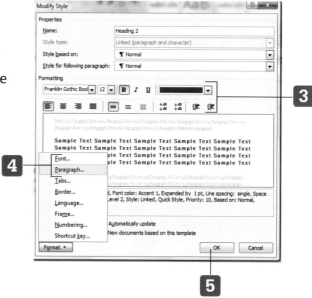

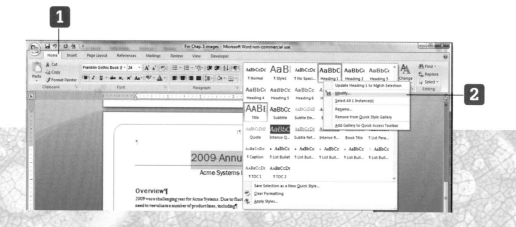

# Create bulleted and numbered lists

Lists give you a useful way to break up long blocks of text and call attention to especially important items or step-by-step instructions. Word makes it easy for you to go beyond a simple single-level list and include lists with many different levels.

**1** Click to position the cursor at the spot in the text where you want to create a list.

**2** Click the Home tab if necessary.

**3** Click the down arrow next to the Bullets or Numbering button in the Styles group, then choose a style from the dropdown menu that appears.

**4** Type the first item in the list, then press Enter. Continue typing your list items in this way until the list is complete.

**5** Click the Bullets or Numbering button again to end the list.

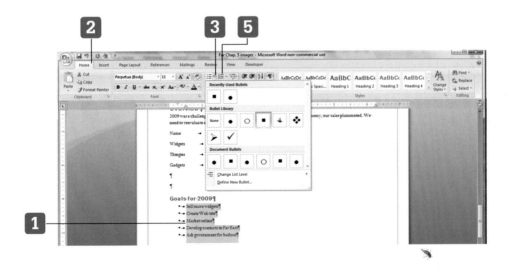

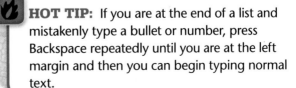

**? DID YOU KNOW?**
To create a sublist within the main list, position the cursor before an item and press the Tab key.

**HOT TIP:** If you are at the end of a list and mistakenly type a bullet or number, press Backspace repeatedly until you are at the left margin and then you can begin typing normal text.

# Modify bullet or number styles

By default, bullets in Word appear as black dots and numbers appear as Roman numerals 1, 2, 3 and so on, but you have many other options to choose from. You can also have a list start at a number other than 1 or change the alignment of list items.

**1** Select the entire list you have created.

**2** Click the Home tab.

**3** Click the down arrow next to the Bullets or Numbering button in the Styles group.

**4** Choose Define New Bullet or Define New Number Format, below the given styles shown.

**5** Change the alignment or choose a graphic object.

**6** Click OK.

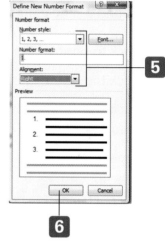

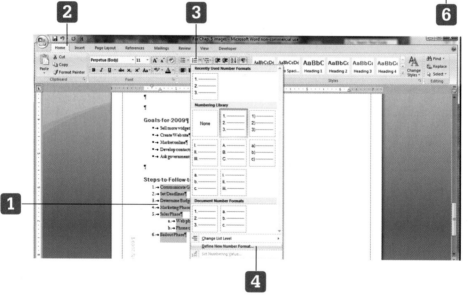

# Create a table

In the previous chapter, you learned how to format tables. Tables arrange data or text in a grid consisting of rows, columns and cells, but how do you create a table in the first place?

The easiest way is to draw the table's layouts. You can also convert text into a table, providing you have separated the text with tabs or into paragraphs.

**1** Select the text that you want to convert into a table.

**2** Click the Insert tab.

**3** Click the Table button, then choose Convert Text to Table, near the bottom of the box.

**4** Alternatively, if you want to draw the table, click and drag over the table cells shown at the top of the box. The cells you select turn dark, so, if you have three rows with three dark cells each, you'll have a table with three rows and three columns.

**5** If you didn't choose the alternative method in step 4, enter the number of rows and columns you want your table to have and choose other formatting as needed.

**6** Click OK when you're happy.

▶ **SEE ALSO:** See Chapter 4 for some quick formatting options for tables.

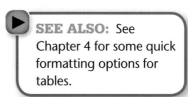

# 6 Working with Excel spreadsheets

# Introduction

Excel 2007 makes it easier than ever to create workbooks and format the worksheets within them. On a worksheet, you can add or remove rows, cells and columns as needed. You can resize and move these elements using Ribbon commands and you can add worksheets or move them by clicking and dragging tabs at the bottom of the Excel window.

Excel, like other Office 2007 applications, is ideally suited to situations when you need to create a framework for data and want to preserve that framework for reasons of consistency while changing the data. The premade templates that come with Excel will be perfect for your business or personal needs.

Some Excel features help you to do your work more efficiently by avoiding trouble. Formula AutoCorrect is an example. When you press the equals sign (=), Formula AutoCorrect is activated. As you type your formula, valid (and correctly spelled) commands appear in a convenient dropdown list.

This chapter describes basic operations that you can perform simply and easily with Excel.

# Select cells

Before you can enter data in a cell, move it or apply a formula to it, you need to select it. Selecting a single cell is easy – you just click it. To select a range, you use Shift + Click, but you can also drag to select cells and use some nifty keyboard shortcuts as well.

**1** Select the first cell in the range by clicking it.

**2** Hold down the Shift key and click the last cell in the range to select all the cells between them. (You can also drag to select a range of contiguous cells.)

**3** Click the first cell or range of cells that you want to select.

**4** Press and hold down the Ctrl key to select other cells in the worksheet that are not contiguous.

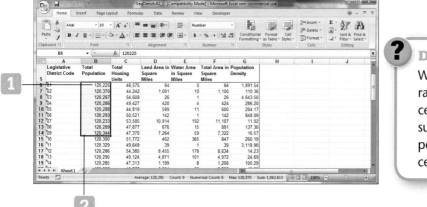

**?** DID YOU KNOW?

When you select a range of contiguous cells, the top-left cell is surrounded by the cell pointer; the rest of the cells are highlighted.

**!** **ALERT:** The Shift + Click method only works if the cells are contiguous. If the cells you want to click are non-contiguous, press and hold down the Ctrl key while selecting the cells.

# Jump to a specific location

The easy way to navigate through the cells in a worksheet is to point your mouse and click. For most situations, this is all you'll need to do. If you have an IntelliMouse or similar, you can move the scroll wheel with your finger to move through cells; the usual pointer changes shape and lets you move through the worksheet as you drag your mouse. Once in a while, though, the Go To dialogue box will help you to get where you're going to faster than this scrolling method.

1 When you want to go to a specific location, click the Home tab.

2 Click Find & Select, then click Go To in the box that appears.

3 Select the location or type a cell address for your destination.

4 Click OK.

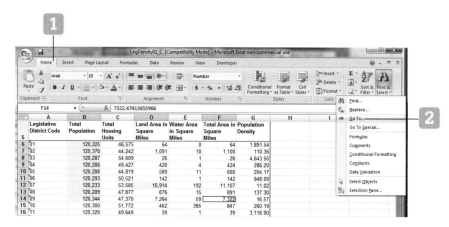

**? DID YOU KNOW?**

If you want to go to comments, the last cell, an object, a formula or another destination not listed in the Go To dialogue box, click Special at the bottom, select a location, then click OK.

# Create labels

Labels are essential for understanding the data in a worksheet. They describe the information contained in rows, columns or individual cells. You don't necessarily have to create a text label, you can use a number as a label if you wish. The AutoComplete feature available with Excel and other Office applications helps you to keep your labels consistent as it enters values based on labels you have used previously.

**1** Click the cell where you want to enter a label.

**2** Type the content for your label.

**3** Press Enter.

**4** To add a number as a label, begin by typing an apostrophe (').

**5** Type the number.

**6** Press Enter.

**? DID YOU KNOW?**

The apostrophe is just a label prefix – it will not appear in your worksheet.

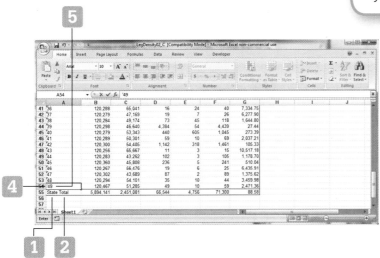

**? DID YOU KNOW?**

A label can contain upper- and lower-case characters, spaces, punctuation and numbers.

# Enter values in a worksheet

Entering values in worksheet cells is one of the basic tasks associated with spreadsheets. Values can take the form of whole numbers, decimals, percentages or dates. You can enter numeric values either using the number keys at the top of your keyboard or pressing the Num Lock key.

**1** Click the cell where you want to enter a value.

**2** Type the value.

**3** Press Enter.

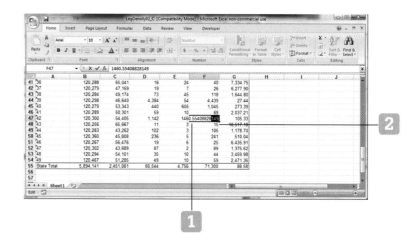

 **HOT TIP:** Rather than pressing the Enter key, you can click the Enter button (the tick) on the formula bar, at the top of the worksheet.

**? DID YOU KNOW?**

When you begin to enter a date or time, Excel recognises the entries (if they correspond to one of its built-in date or time formats) and changes the information to fit its default date or time format.

# Edit cell contents

One of the best things about Excel worksheets is the fact that they can be quickly updated. Making changes to cells is easy, but the process differs slightly from that used to enter data.

**1** Double-click the cell you want to edit. The insertion point appears within the cell, and the status bar displays Edit instead of Ready.

**2** If you need to move the insertion point inside the cell, use the arrow, Home or End keys.

**3** Press Backspace or the Delete (Del) key to remove characters as needed, then type in the new ones.

**4** Do one of the following to end editing:

- Press Enter.

- Press the Esc key.

The status bar changes back to Ready instead of Edit.

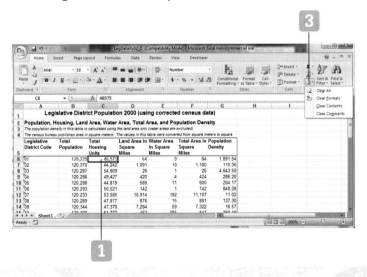

# Clear cell contents

When you first start using Excel, you might think clearing a cell's contents is a simple matter of pressing the Backspace or Delete key, but Excel 2007 gives you control over exactly what you want to clear. In case you have applied formatting to a cell and you want to keep the formatting, even as you cut the data, Excel lets you do so.

**1** Click to select the cell or range of cells that you want to clear.

**2** Click the Home tab if necessary.

**3** Click the Clear button, then choose one of the following:

- Clear All – to clear both contents and formatting
- Clear Formats – to clear formatting, but leave the contents
- Clear Contents – to clear contents and leave the formatting
- Clear Comments – to clear comments that you have made relating to those cells.

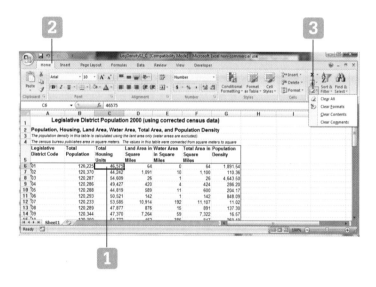

**HOT TIP:** To clear contents faster, right-click the contents and choose Clear Contents from the context menu.

# Select rows, columns and special ranges

You now know how to select a single cell or a range of cells – or even a non-contiguous set of cells. Sometimes when working with Excel, you'll need to select entire rows or columns, entire worksheets or ranges that span multiple worksheets. If such a need arises, try the techniques described in this task.

1 To select an entire row or column, click to select a cell anywhere in the column, then press Shift + spacebar.

2 After you have selected a row or column, if you need to select other, non-adjacent rows or columns, press and hold down Ctrl while you click anywhere in the borders for the other columns you want.

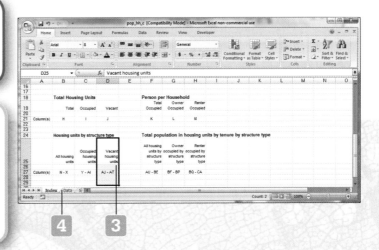

3 To select a multisheet range, select the range in one sheet.

4 Select the worksheet tabs at the bottom of the Excel window to choose the worksheets you want to include in the same range.

▶ **SEE ALSO:** See Select cells at the beginning of this chapter for some tips on selecting groups of cells.

? **DID YOU KNOW?**

If you have selected an entire row or column and you need to select adjacent rows or columns, drag over the adjacent row or column headings.

# Name a worksheet

Each Excel workbook opens with three worksheets in which you can work with information. The default worksheet names are the generic designations of Sheet1, Sheet2 and Sheet3. Whenever you need to add a worksheet, click the Insert Worksheet tab at the bottom of the window. You can then name your new worksheet – or change the generic names of other sheets to more recognisable ones – with just a few steps.

**1** To select a worksheet, click one of the tabs at the bottom of the open worksheet.

**2** To add a new worksheet, click the Insert Worksheet symbol tab, next to the last worksheet tab.

**3** To name a worksheet, double-click its sheet tab.

**4** Type a new name.

**5** Press Enter.

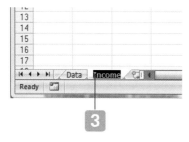

**3**

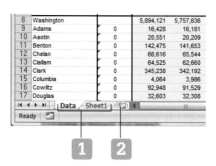

**1**  **2**

 **HOT TIP:** To select all the worksheets at once, right-click any sheet tab, then choose Select All Sheets.

# Delete a worksheet

Sometimes, you end up with more worksheet space than you have information. To keep file sizes small and your workbooks manageable, delete any unneeded sheets.

**1** Click the tab of the sheet you want to remove.

**2** Click the Home tab, if necessary.

**3** Click the Delete button down arrow in the Cells group of buttons and choose Delete Sheet from the options that pop up.

**4** Click Delete to confirm the operation.

**HOT TIP:** You can also right-click the sheet tab and choose Delete from the context menu to quickly remove a sheet.

# Move or copy a worksheet

After you have assembled your data, you might need to reorder the worksheets to fit a particular pattern – to put them in chronological order, for instance. You can either copy a worksheet to the new location and then delete the previous version or else simply move the sheet from one place to another. In either case, Excel 2007 makes the task easy.

**1** Click the tab of the worksheet you want to copy.

**2** Click the Home tab.

**3** Click the Format button down arrow in the Cells group of buttons and choose Move or Copy Sheet in the box that pops up.

**4** To copy the sheet to another workbook that you have open, click the To book dropdown list and choose the name of the workbook.

**5** To copy the sheet to another location in the current workbook, choose another sheet from the list in the Before sheet box.

**6** Click OK.

**? DID YOU KNOW?**

When you copy a worksheet to another location in the same workbook, Excel places it to the left (before) the sheet you choose.

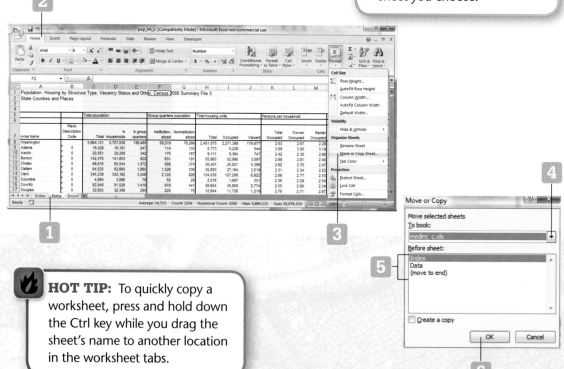

**HOT TIP:** To quickly copy a worksheet, press and hold down the Ctrl key while you drag the sheet's name to another location in the worksheet tabs.

# Insert a column or row

When you add a new blank column or row to a worksheet, Excel preserves the existing columns and rows as well as any formulas that apply to them. Formulas that make absolute (rather than relative) references to cells, however, will need to be adjusted manually.

When you insert a column, it is placed to the left of the column you select. When you insert a row, it goes above the row you select.

**1** Click anywhere to the right of where you want the new column to go, or immediately below the row you want the new row to sit under.

**2** Click the Home tab.

**3** Click the Insert down arrow in the Cells group of buttons, then choose Insert Sheet Columns or Insert Sheet Rows from the box that appears.

**4** If you need to adjust the formatting, click the Insert Options button just below and to the right of the element you inserted and choose a formatting option.

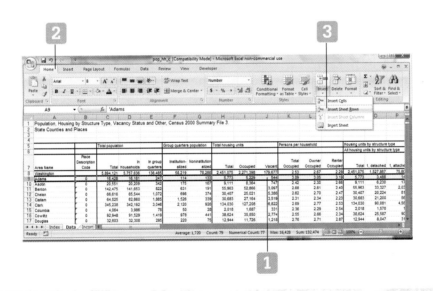

## DID YOU KNOW?

You can insert more than one column or row at a time. First, drag to select the row header buttons or column header buttons that correspond to the number of columns or rows you want to add. If you want to insert two rows above row 18, select rows 18 and 19, for instance. Then, click Insert and choose Insert Sheet Columns or Insert Sheet Rows as needed.

# Delete a column or row

In the course of editing data, you may need to remove a whole row or column rather than a cell or group of cells. The process is similar to that used to insert rows or columns. The remaining columns will be moved either to the left or up to join the rest of the data.

**1** Select the header button of the column or row you want to delete.

**2** Click the Home tab.

**3** Click the Delete button in the Cells group and then choose Delete Sheet Columns or Delete Sheet Rows.

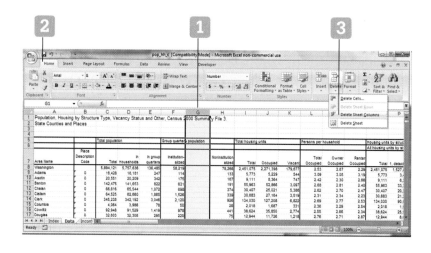

**? DID YOU KNOW?**

You can select multiple header buttons for columns or rows if you need to delete multiple items.

**! ALERT:** Make sure that you check formulas in your worksheet before you delete a row or column. You might not want to delete formulas that make absolute references to the cells you are about to delete.

# Adjust column or row size

Once you have entered data in your worksheet, you'll probably need to do some formatting. Adjusting the width of columns and the height of rows makes your information more readable, especially if some of your data isn't visible in its entirety. It also happens that most labels turn out larger than the standard width of a column, so you need to widen the columns to make them visible.

You can easily change the default size of both rows and columns to accommodate your labels and data.

**1** Click the column or row header of the column or row that you need to adjust.

**2** Optionally, you can select more columns or rows if you need to adjust them all at once.

**3** Click the Home tab if needed.

**4** Click the Format button in the Cells group and choose Column Width or Row Height.

**5** Type the new column width or row height in points.

**6** Click OK.

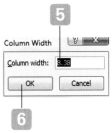

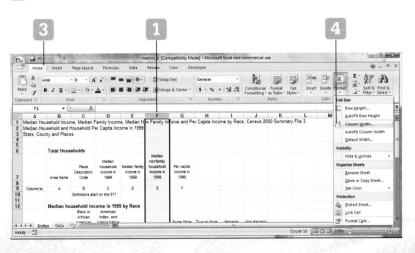

**? DID YOU KNOW?**
One centimetre equals 28.8 points.

**🔥 HOT TIP:** You can also right-click the selected column or row and choose Column Width or Row Height from the context menu.

# Divide a worksheet into panes

If you are working with a worksheet that contains many computer screens' worth of data, you can't see the entire contents at once. Rather than having to scroll up and down between different parts of the file, you can divide it into four panes. That way you can scroll independently through each of the two parts of the worksheet and work with both parts at once.

**1** Click a cell, column or row to select the area of the file at the point where you want to create the separate panes.

**2** Click the View tab.

**3** Click Split in the Window group of buttons.

**4** If you want to remove the split and return to one pane, click the Split button again.

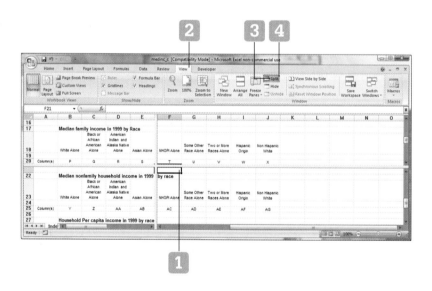

---

**? DID YOU KNOW?**

If you select a cell, you split the worksheet into four panes. If you select a row or column, you divide it in two.

**? DID YOU KNOW?**

Once you have two panes, you can resize them by dragging the drag bar at the bottom right-hand corner of the Excel window or by clicking and dragging the pane divider up and down.

# Create a basic formula

Formulas are powerful features of Excel worksheets. They calculate values you have entered and return results for you. Excel provides you with a set of operators that you can use to perform addition, multiplication, division and other calculations. Each formula starts with an argument: the cell references or values that combine to produce a result. If your formula is long, you can resize the formula bar to accommodate it.

**1** Click the cell that you want to contain the formula.

**2** Type the equals sign (=) to begin so Excel will calculate the values you enter. (If you don't, Excel will simply display what you type.)

**3** Enter the first argument – a number or a cell reference.

**4** Enter an operator such as the asterisk (*) for multiplication.

**5** Enter the next argument and repeat values and operators as needed.

**6** Press Enter or click the Enter button (the tick) on the formula bar. The result appears in the cell.

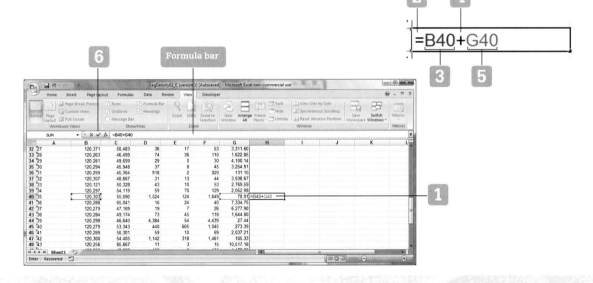

**HOT TIP:** Pointing to a cell rather than typing its address reduces the chances of typing errors.

**? DID YOU KNOW?**
By default, only formula results are displayed in a cell, but you can adjust the worksheet view to display the formula itself.

# Display formulas

By default, formulas aren't displayed in your worksheet cells. When you press Enter or click the Enter button on the formula bar, the calculation you have specified is performed. You may want to display formulas in the cells rather than automatically calculating them, however. Do so by following these steps.

1 Click the Formulas tab.

2 Click Show Formulas in the Formula Auditing group of buttons.

3 Click the Show Formulas button again to disable the display of formulas.

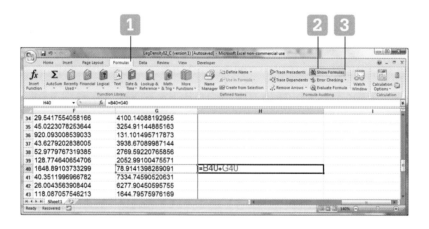

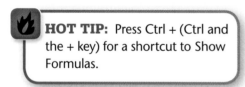

**HOT TIP:** Press Ctrl + (Ctrl and the + key) for a shortcut to Show Formulas.

# Use Formula AutoComplete

One of Excel 2007's most useful new features is Formula AutoComplete. It provides you with suggestions for valid functions, arguments, defined names and other items that help you to accurately complete a formula without typing everything from scratch. Whenever you type a text string, a dropdown list appears with items that will help you complete your typing.

**1** Click the cell where you want to enter the formula.

**2** Type = (the equals sign) and some beginning letters of a formula to start Formula AutoComplete.

**3** Scan the list of valid items, which will change if you continue to type.

**4** Press Tab or double-click an item to select it.

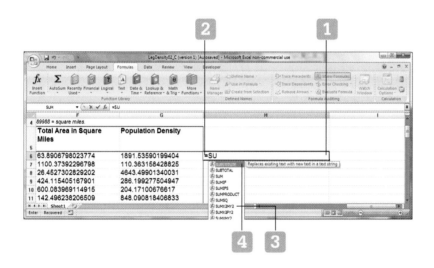

<hr />

**?** **DID YOU KNOW?**

The text just before the cursor determines what appears in the Formula AutoComplete dropdown list.

**?** **DID YOU KNOW?**

You may need to turn on Formula AutoComplete. If so, click the Office button, click Excel Options, click Formulas on the left-hand side, click the Formula AutoComplete tick box and click OK.

# Edit a formula

It's not difficult to edit a formula, especially as the formula bar just above your worksheet data is available for this purpose. There are a couple of tricks you need to perform, though, in order to enter edit mode and be able to make the necessary changes.

**1** Select the cell that contains the formula you need to edit.

**2** Press F2 to enter Edit mode.

**3** Use the Home, End and arrow keys to move through the formula so that you can make your edits.

**4** Press Backspace or Del (Delete) to remove items so that you can make corrections.

**5** When you've finished, click Enter on the formula bar or press Enter.

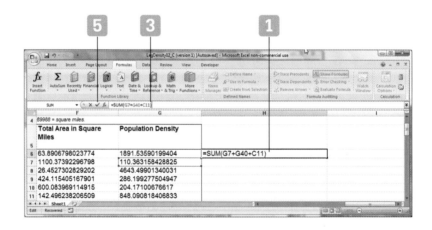

# Apply conditional formatting

Conditional formatting gives you a way to indicate a cell's value by displaying special formatting. For example, you can make numerals less than zero display in red. You can have especially high sales figures highlighted in green and bold. The formatting, therefore, is used only if the value meets criteria you specify.

1 Select the cell or range of cells that you want to format using the conditions you specify.

2 Click the Home tab if necessary.

3 Click Conditional Formatting in the Styles group of buttons and point to Highlight Cell Rules in the box that appears.

4 Click a rule that you want to specify as part of your conditional formatting in the submenu.

5 Enter the criteria you want.

6 Click OK.

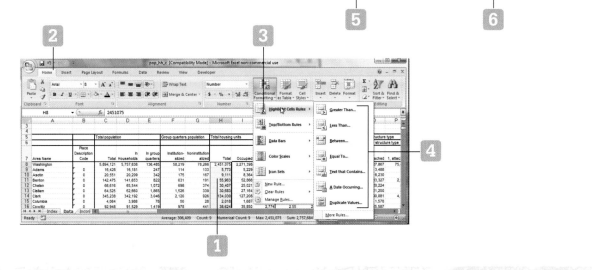

**DID YOU KNOW?**

You can apply conditional formatting only to cells that contain text, number or date or time values.

# 7 Assembling PowerPoint presentations

# Introduction

PowerPoint presentations need to look good as the purpose of such presentations is to share them with others – often in a classroom or a business environment – so you need to take care with how your words and images appear. Fortunately for you, PowerPoint 2007 gives you the tools you need. These include lists, images, charts, tables and multimedia clips. You can move objects freely from one part of a presentation to another as you assemble your work.

Like other Office 2007 applications, PowerPoint provides you with an AutoCorrect feature that minimises typographical errors. Built-in thesaurus and dictionary help you to choose the right words. An Outline pane gives you a place to make notes that will help you to edit your presentation at a later date.

After you gather the words and images and arrange them on slides, you need to consider how best to present them. You'll find PowerPoint 2007's navigation tools helpful when moving around your presentation. As you make the presentation, you can use your mouse as a pointer. You can also add notes to your slideshow to highlight important points for your viewers and store your presentation as a compressed file or save it on CD so that you can use it any time you wish.

# Navigate a presentation

PowerPoint presentations give you a number of shortcuts that you can use to find your way around a presentation quickly. In addition, some buttons in the PowerPoint window perform special functions that can be timesavers.

**1** Click the Up or Down arrows on the right of the screen to scroll line by line.

**2** Click the Previous Slide and Next Slide buttons to move a whole slide at a time.

**3** Click one of the thumbnails in the Slides pane on the left to jump to that slide.

**4** Use the scroll bar next to the Slides pane to view the thumbnails quickly.

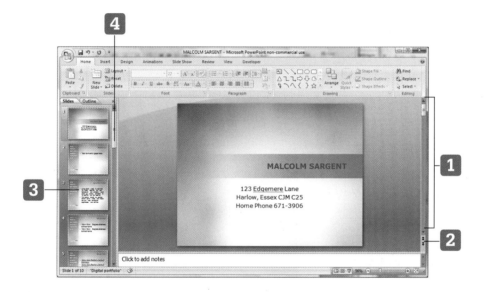

 **HOT TIP:** Press the PgUp or PgDown buttons at each end of the slider on the right of the screen to move between slides one at a time.

# Switch views

PowerPoint, like Word and Excel, gives you different ways to view information – the default view is just one of several options. Take a moment to browse through the other options so that you know what's available. When it is time to put the finishing touches to your slideshow, you'll be happy to use Slide Sorter or Slide Show view, for instance.

**1** To switch from one view to another, do one of the following:

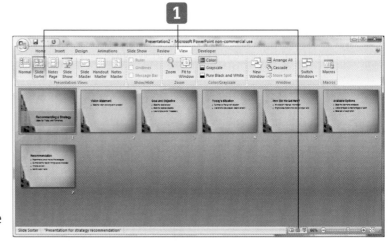

- Click the View tab, then one of the options in the Presentation Views group of buttons

- Click one of the view buttons in the status bar.

The available options are:

- Normal View – contains the outline, slide and notes in their own panes

- Slide Sorter – provides you with transitions and animations that help you to move from one slide to another

- Slide Show – displays your slides one at a time.

**Recommending a Strategy**
Ideas for Today and Tomorrow

 **HOT TIP:** Press the Esc key to leave Slide Show view.

# Create a new slide

Whether you want to create a new blank slide or apply an existing slide's formatting to a new one, PowerPoint makes it easy to do so. The tools are especially effective when it comes to creating a consistent appearance throughout a presentation. Any slide layout contains placeholders for images, text, charts and other objects.

**1** Click the Home tab if needed.

**2** Click the down arrow next to New Slide in the Slides group of buttons.

**3** Choose the layout you want from the slide layout gallery.

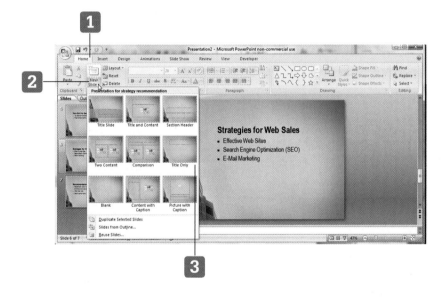

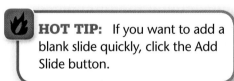

**HOT TIP:** If you want to add a blank slide quickly, click the Add Slide button.

# Change a slide's layout

Once you insert a slide, you can apply one of a group of predetermined layouts to it. The layouts have colour, type and the general arrangement already set. You can also apply a customised layout – one you have prepared yourself.

**1** Make sure you are in Normal view (select from the icons at the bottom of the screen).

**2** Click the Home tab.

**3** Click the Layout button in the Slides group, then choose the layout you want from the options that pop up.

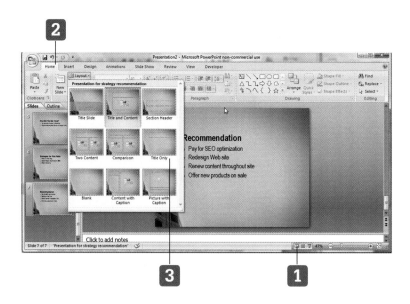

**? DID YOU KNOW?**

When you change the layout of a slide, PowerPoint keeps the existing information and adds the new look.

**? DID YOU KNOW?**

You can duplicate a slide. In the Slides pane or in Slide Sorter view, select the slide you want to duplicate. Click Home, Click the New Slide button in the Slides group, and click Duplicate Selected Slides.

# Work with objects

Once you have added a text block, image, chart or other object to a slide, you can easily move, copy or resize it. Before you perform any action on an object, however, you first need to select it. An object that has been selected is outlined by a rectangle called a selection box that has sizing handles at the sides and corners.

**1** Select an object by moving the pointer over it and clicking it.

**2** Move the object by hovering the pointer over it (it becomes a four-headed arrow) and dragging with the mouse.

**3** To resize the object, click and drag one of the sizing handles; to constrain the original shape, so that you can resize it equally in all dimensions, press Shift while you drag.

**4** To deselect the object, click anywhere outside its boundaries.

**? DID YOU KNOW?**

When your pointer is over an object and it can be clicked, the pointer changes to a four-headed arrow.

**? DID YOU KNOW?**

To copy the object, press and hold down the Ctrl key while dragging.

# Insert a template

If you don't want to create a presentation from scratch, turn to the templates that Office 2007 provides for you. PowerPoint comes with a selection of pre-installed templates. If you don't find the one you want, you'll find a wide selection on Microsoft Office Online. You can choose templates for everything from invitations to agendas. By starting with a template, you get a suggested set of slides that you can modify to fit your own needs.

**1** Click the Office button.

**2** Click New.

**3** Click Installed Templates to view the templates that come with PowerPoint.

**4** Click one of the categories under Microsoft Office Online to view templates online.

**5** Select the template you want.

**6** Click Create.

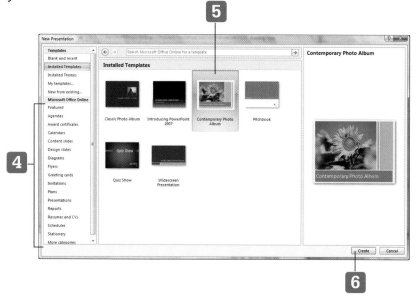

**!** **ALERT:** Some of the templates at Microsoft Office Online were submitted by individuals rather than Microsoft itself. Make sure that there aren't any permissions issues before you copy a template.

**?** **DID YOU KNOW?**

To download the Microsoft Office Online templates, you need to use Internet Explorer and an Active X control may have to be installed so that you can view and install the template you want.

# Use text placeholders

If you're used to entering text in Word or even in an Excel worksheet, you're used to simply positioning the cursor and typing. In PowerPoint, text is treated as an object, like images and charts. When you insert one of PowerPoint's templates, text is provided in a box with a dashed line around it – a placeholder – that you then replace with your own content.

**1** Make sure you are in Normal view.

**2** Click the text placeholder once to select it.

**3** Type the text you want to enter.

**4** Click anywhere outside the text box to deselect it.

Text placeholder

# Select and modify text

After you have created text in PowerPoint, it is contained in a box with sizing handles, just like an image. This makes it easy to move and modify the text as well as enter it.

1. Click once to select the placeholder.

2. Click inside the placeholder to position the insertion point.

3. Double-click to select a word or press Backspace or Del to delete text so that you can type new content.

4. Click anywhere outside the box to deselect it.

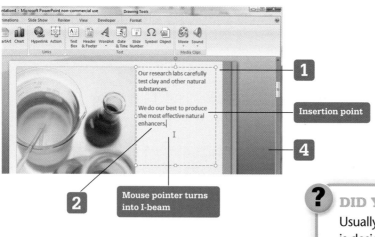

**1**

**Insertion point**

**4**

**2**

**Mouse pointer turns into I-beam**

**? DID YOU KNOW?**

Usually, the insertion point is designated by a blinking vertical line or cursor. When you click to create a text box, the insertion point changes to an I-beam. When the I-beam is present you can click, type and edit text.

# Create a list

Bulleted and numbered lists are important parts of nearly every PowerPoint presentation. They present information in a compact way and give the presenter a natural set of talking points that can be covered while giving a talk about a subject.

**1** Make sure that you are in Normal view, and click the Home tab.

**2** Position the text cursor at the point where you want the list to begin.

**3** Click the Bullets or Numbering button in the Paragraph group.

**4** Type the first list item, then press Enter.

**5** Type the second item.

**6** Repeat steps 4 and 5 until the list is complete.

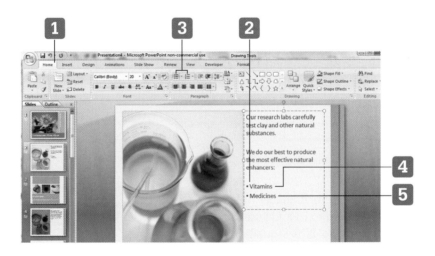

---

**?** **DID YOU KNOW?**

You can increase the list level so that the list is idented further to the right and has a different system before each item. Press the Tab key or click the Increase List Level button on the Home tab. To decrease the level, press Shift + Tab or click the Decrease List Level button on the Home tab.

**HOT TIP:** Make sure that you press the spacebar once to separate the bullet or number from the item that follows it.

# Take advantage of AutoFit

One of the nice features of PowerPoint 2007 is the ability to automatically fit text to the size of the available text box. This maximises the visibility of your text on a screen when you are giving a presentation. AutoFit means that you don't have to change the size manually.

**1** To turn on AutoFit, click the Office button.

**2** Choose PowerPoint Options at the bottom of the box.

**3** Click Proofing, then AutoCorrect Options.

**4** Click the AutoFormat As You Type tab.

**5** Tick the AutoFit title next to placeholder and AutoFit body text to placeholder tick boxes.

**6** Click OK.

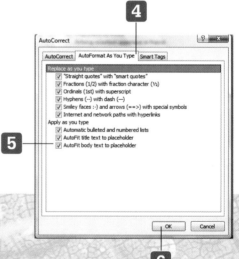

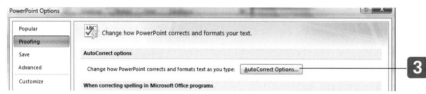

**?** **DID YOU KNOW?**

If you don't like the AutoFit feature (it takes some time to get used to it) and you want to turn it off, use the AutoFit dialogue box to do so: untick the AutoFit title text to placeholder and AutoFit body text to placeholder tick boxes in the AutoFormat As You Type dialogue box.

# Develop an outline

Outlines are useful for not only organising your thoughts but also giving a presentation. You can easily develop your own outline from scratch in the Outline pane or insert one from a presentation or document that you have already made.

**1** Click in the Outline pane to position the cursor where you want the outline to appear.

**2** Type the outline title and press Enter.

**3** To indent the next item to the right a level, press Tab before typing.

**4** When you want to insert a slide in the Outline pane, click the New Slide button in the Slides group and then choose a layout.

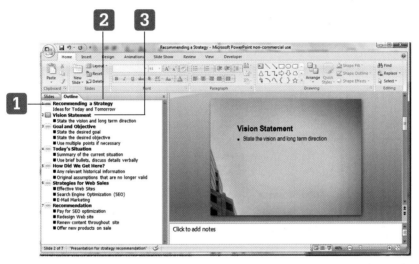

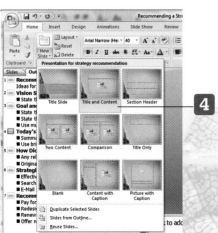

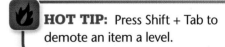

**HOT TIP:** Press Shift + Tab to demote an item a level.

**DID YOU KNOW?**

You can insert an outline you created from another Office application, such as Word. Click the New Slide down arrow, choose Slides from Outline, locate the outline file, then click Insert.

# Duplicate a slide

When you are creating a presentation or editing one, you don't need to begin every slide from scratch. If you have a slide with the layout, type and colour configuration you want, you can duplicate it with a few mouse clicks.

**1** In Normal view, click the slide you want to duplicate in the Outline pane.

**2** Click the Home tab.

**3** Click the New Slide down arrow in the Slides group.

**4** Click Duplicate Selected Slides.

**?** **DID YOU KNOW?**

You can duplicate multiple slides at once. To select slides in a sequence, click the first one, pressing and holding down Shift, then select the last one. To select slides that are not in sequence, press and hold Ctrl and click the ones you want.

# Manage slides with Slide Sorter

Slide Sorter view gives you an effective way to get an overview of all the slides in a presentation. You can use this view to rearrange slides, dragging and dropping them until they are where you want them.

1. Click the View tab.

2. Click Slide Sorter view in the Presentation Views group of buttons.

3. Click the slide you want to move and hold down the mouse button.

4. Drag the slide to a new location.

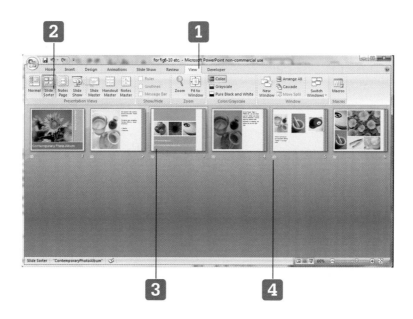

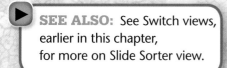

**SEE ALSO:** See Switch views, earlier in this chapter, for more on Slide Sorter view.

**? DID YOU KNOW?**
A vertical line appears where the slide will be moved to when you release the mouse button.

# Import slides

You can bring slides into the presentation you're assembling by either copying and pasting them or using a new feature called the Reuse Slides task pane. The advantage of the Reuse task pane is that you don't have to have the previous presentation (the one from which you are taking the slides) open first.

**1** Click the Home tab if necessary.

**2** Click the New Slide down arrow in the Slides group and choose Reuse Slides at the bottom of the box of options.

**3** In the Reuse Slides task pane, click Browse, choose Browse File, select the file you want, and click Open.

**4** Select the slide you want to import.

**5** Click Close to close the task pane.

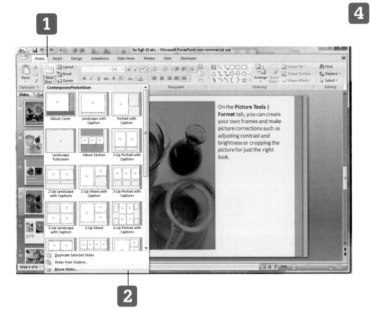

**HOT TIP:** To insert all the slides at once from a file, right-click any slide and choose Insert All Slides.

# Insert a slide master

Slide Master creates a container for objects such as logos or text-based slogans that you want to appear on each slide in your presentation. Slide Master includes controls that let you delete, rename or copy masters. You can lock a master to keep it from being deleted.

**1** Click the View tab.

**2** Click the Slide Master button in the Presentation Views group.

**3** Click the Insert tab to add objects or type text on the master.

**4** Click Colors, Themes, Fonts or other controls to edit the theme of the master slide, when on the Slide Master tab.

**5** When you've finished, click the Close Master View button.

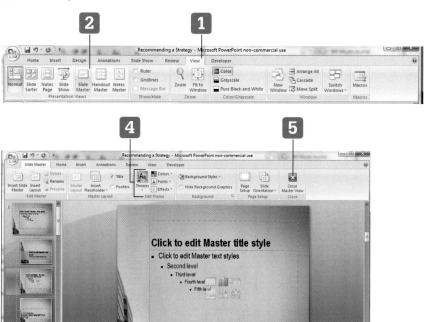

**? DID YOU KNOW?**

When you insert Slide Master, it is added just beneath the currently displayed slide.

# Insert placeholder content

Slide Master includes a set of layouts that you can choose from. In order to customise the layout, you can add content in the form of placeholders. You can add content, text, picture, chart, table, diagram, media or clip art placeholders. The content will then appear on each slide in your presentation.

**1** Click View and choose Slide Master to open the Slide Master tab.

**2** Choose the layout you want from the Slide Master pane, on the left of the screen.

**3** Click the Insert Layout button in the Edit Master group to associate a new layout with Slide Master.

**4** Click the down arrow next to Insert Placeholder in the Master Layout group and click the type of placeholder you want to add from the option in the box that appears.

**5** Click and drag to create a placeholder on the slide layout.

**6** When you're happy, click the Close Master View button, top right.

**? DID YOU KNOW?**

You can simply click the Insert Placeholder button rather than clicking the down arrow on the right side of it. This adds a generic placeholder that can hold any kind of content.

# Change the page setup

If you ever need to print out a presentation, you need to first make sure that it will appear how you want. By default, PowerPoint uses landscape orientation and starts slides at number one. To check the overall printed page size and the orientation of each page, open the Page Setup dialogue box.

**1** Click the Design tab.

**2** Click Page Setup in the Page Setup group of buttons.

**3** Choose an option from the dropdown list that appears to specify the height-to-width proportion for slides in your presentation.

**4** Specify the width and height of each slide.

**5** Choose Portrait or Landscape orientation.

**6** Click OK.

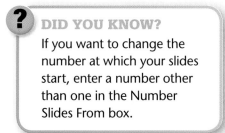

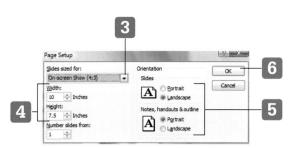

**? DID YOU KNOW?**

If you want to change the number at which your slides start, enter a number other than one in the Number Slides From box.

**! ALERT:** The Design tab does not appear if the Slide Master tab is open. Close the Slide Master tab if necessary.

# Adjust slide timing

When you play a presentation as a slide show, it's important to adjust the timing between slides to make sure that the presentation goes by at the optimal speed.

**1** Click the Slide Show tab.

**2** Click the Rehearse Timings button.

**3** As the time goes by in the Rehearsal dialogue box, press Enter to move from one slide to the next.

**4** When you are done and a confirmation dialogue box appears, click Yes to accept the timings.

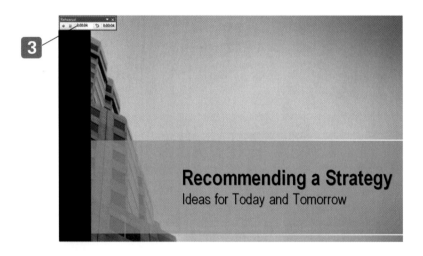

**Recommending a Strategy**
Ideas for Today and Tomorrow

# Edit slide timing

If you need to change the length of time a slide or slides show for, you can use the Animations tab – one of several new tabs that have become available in Slide Sorter view.

**1** To edit slide timings, switch to Slide Sorter view.

**2** Click the slide or slides for which you want to change the timings.

**3** Click the Animations tab.

**4** Type a new value in the seconds box.

**5** Press Enter to save the new timing or timings.

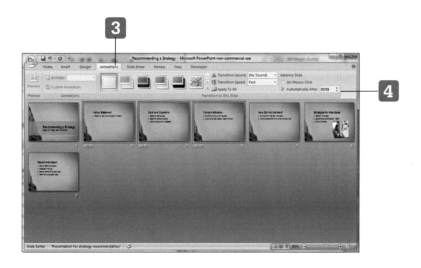

# 8 Creating an Access database

# Introduction

Many of the Office 2007 applications discussed in preceding chapters help you to organise information, but nothing allows you to organise the way Access 2007 does. Access has the capacity to store huge amounts of data in a highly organised database structure that makes it easy to find and retrieve. You can also create forms that allow you to enter information into a database.

You don't need to be highly experienced with databases to use Access, either. Like other Office 2007 applications, Access comes with templates that you can use for personal, business, or other purposes. If you want to edit a database created in an earlier version of Access or other programs, you'll find it easy to do so.

This chapter introduces you to some of the many basic database functions that you can perform with Access. You don't need to climb a steep learning curve and master complex database design to start working with data. You'll learn how to create a database, view data, enter new data and print out reports that help you and your colleagues to interpret the information you've assembled.

# Use a template to create a database

The simplest way to create an Access database is to use one of the templates that come with the application. Templates contain all the elements you need to organise data, including fields, tables, queries, reports and forms.

**1** Click the Office button.

**2** Choose New. The Getting Started with Microsoft Access 2007 dialogue box opens.

**3** Click the type of template that you want to use in the Template Categories pane. You can search through templates installed with Access (Featuring or Local Templates) or, if you are connected to the Internet, those provided on Microsoft Office Online.

**4** Click the specific template you want.

**5** Click the Browse button, click the Save in down arrow and save the file on your computer.

**6** Click Create.

> **⚠ ALERT:** If a security dialogue box appears, click Options, click Enable this content, then click OK.

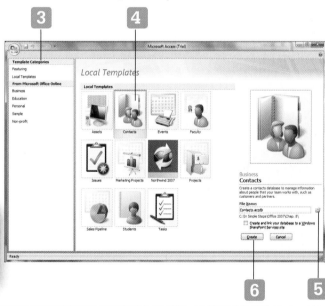

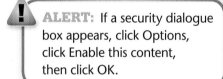

---

**❓ DID YOU KNOW?**

An Access database consists of several different elements, including:

- Forms – let you enter information into a database
- Tables – contain a set of data about a topic, each contained in a separate field
- Queries – give you a way to locate information stored in a database
- Reports – are summaries of the data stored in a database
- Macros – are programs that provide a single shortcut for a series of actions that you need to perform
- Modules – are programs that extend the functionality of a database.

# Assemble a blank database

If Access templates don't cover your needs or if you need to create a customised database, you can quickly do so from scratch. You just need to name your file and save it in a location where you can find it easily.

**1** Click the Office button.

**2** Click New.

**3** Click Featuring in the Template Categories pane.

**4** Click Blank Database in the box that appears.

**5** If necessary, click the Browse button, click the Save in down arrow and click OK to choose a location for your file.

**6** Type a name for your file, then click Create.

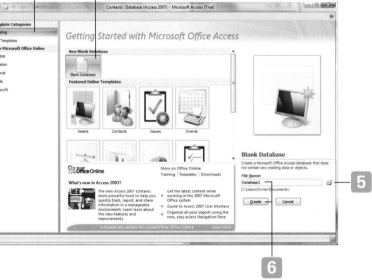

**? DID YOU KNOW?**

You can save a database file in the .mdb format used by Access 2000 or 2002–2003, or else the .accdb format used by Access 2007.

# Work with the Access window

Once you have created a new database, you need to start working with the parts of the Access window that help you to manipulate and store data.

Access 2007 presents you with the same Ribbon-based interface that you see in other Office 2007 applications, but it also includes a set of tabs that displays tables, queries, forms, reports and macros. The Navigation pane shows you the database objects that you currently have.

**1** Click the Save button in the Quick Access Toolbar periodically to save your work.

**2** Click the double arrows to display or hide the Navigation pane.

**3** Click the tabs to the right of the Navigation pane to view the objects that you can work with in the currently open database.

**4** Click one of the View buttons at the bottom right of the screen to move from one view to another:

- Form view
- Datasheet view
- Layout view
- Design view.

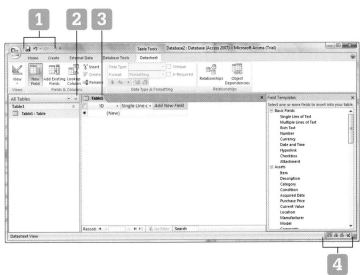

---

 **DID YOU KNOW?**

Another element of the Access interface, a Switchboard, is a window that lets you easily access common actions that you might need to make.

# Customise Access display options

You can change what appears in the Access window by customising the program's display options. Not only that, but you can customise the options that appear in a specific database. You can also display the form you want to appear on startup.

**1** Click the Office button and choose Access Options.

**2** Click Current Database in the left pane.

**3** Enter a database application title.

**4** Choose the form object you want to display on startup.

**5** Check or clear the display options you want.

**6** Click OK.

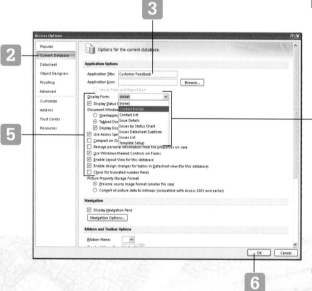

**? DID YOU KNOW?**

A feature new to Access 2007, Layout view, lets you change the design of a form or report while you view it.

**? DID YOU KNOW?**

Access Options let you display your database objects as a set of tabbed documents that you can easily access or as overlapping windows.

# Add fields from templates

Even if you choose to create a blank database file from scratch, Access is there to provide help if you need it. A generic Add New Field object is added and highlighted so that you can replace it with a specific type of field if you want to.

When the database opens, a set of commonly used field templates is provided for you. A 'field template' is a predesigned field with a name, data type, length and other preset properties. You can choose the templates and add them to your file or create your own generic fields.

1. To create a blank field, choose a general type of field from the Basic Fields list at the top of the Field Templates pane on the right of the screen.

2. If you need a specific type of field, scroll down the categories in the Field Templates pane to find one that fits your needs.

3. Drag the field you want into the datasheet and release the mouse button.

**DID YOU KNOW?**

Open the Navigation pane and choose a table to which you want to add a field. When you open a table, the Table Tools tab appears in the Ribbon. Click the Datasheet tab to view Field Templates.

**DID YOU KNOW?**

When you drag a field into the datasheet, you need to position it between the headers of existing fields.

# Reuse existing fields

If you are working with a template or an existing database, you will probably want to reuse fields that already exist in the file. Access 2007 makes it easy to do so – just choose one of the existing fields from the Field List and drag it into the datasheet to use it.

**1** Open the Navigation pane.

**2** Click the table to which you want to add a field.

**3** Click the Add Existing Fields button in the Fields & Columns group.

**4** Click and drag one of the fields already included in the active table in the datasheet, shown in the Field List on the right of the screen.

**5** Click and drag one of the other fields in the database, shown in the list below the one just clicked.

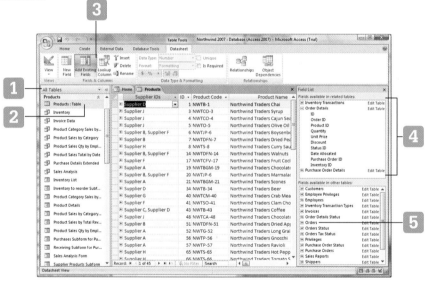

**? DID YOU KNOW?**

Specific types of fields, such as the Total Row, let you perform calculations such as sum, count, average or maximum or minimum.

# Explore database objects

Every Access database contains up to seven different types of objects. Each object, together with the others, constitutes a complete picture of the data you have stored. You locate and move between the different database objects in the Navigation pane on the left side of the Access window. The Navigation pane also includes a dropdown list. The dropdown list lets you view database contents by categories and groups. Click the down arrow at the top of the Navigation pane and you can view predefined and customised categories for the currently open database: the upper section lists the categories and the lower section lists predefined and customised groups for the categories.

**1** Open the database file that you want to work with.

**2** Click the Open/Close button to open the Navigation pane fully, if needed.

**3** Double-click the button for the object you want to view.

**4** Click the down arrow at the top of the Navigation pane.

**5** Click a category.

**6** Click a group.

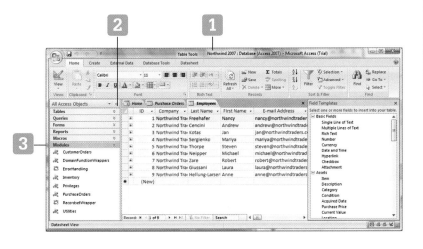

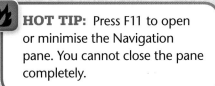

**HOT TIP:** Press F11 to open or minimise the Navigation pane. You cannot close the pane completely.

**DID YOU KNOW?**

The Navigation pane replaces the Database window used in earlier versions of Access.

# Manage database objects

The objects that make up a database are there to help you track and work with your data, but you don't have to stick with the default names for objects. You can create new objects, hide some objects or delete them. That way, each database will have only the selection of objects that you need.

**1** Double-click an object in the Navigation pane to open it or right-click the object to change its design.

**2** Choose Delete from the context menu to delete the object.

**3** Click the Create tab.

**4** Click the button for the type of object you want to create.

**5** Work with the object when it opens in the Reading pane.

**6** Click the Object's Close button when you have finished.

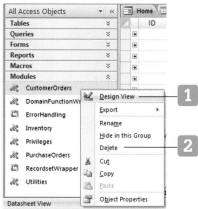

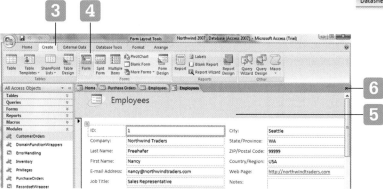

 **DID YOU KNOW?**

The AutoCorrect feature automatically renames objects. When you rename an object, any subsequent objects that use the object you have just renamed are given that name as well. Click the Office button, click Access Options, click Current Database, then select the Name AutoCorrect options you want.

# Create a table with a template

Tables are grids that let you store and work with data. You can create a new table at any time using one of the templates Access gives you.

A table template includes predefined fields that you can enter data into and which can serve specific functions. The available templates include tables for Contacts, Tasks, Issues, Events and Assets. Once you have added a table template using the Create tab, you can edit it to suit your database needs.

**1** Click the Create tab.

**2** Click the Table Templates button in the Tables group.

**3** Choose the type of template you want from the dropdown list that appears.

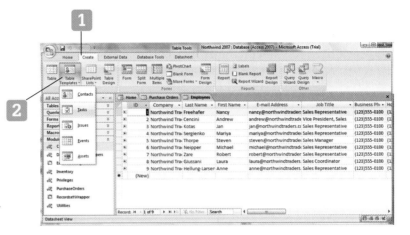

**4** Edit a field's name by double-clicking the placeholder name, typing the new one, then pressing Enter.

**5** Click Save.

**6** Type a name for your table and click OK.

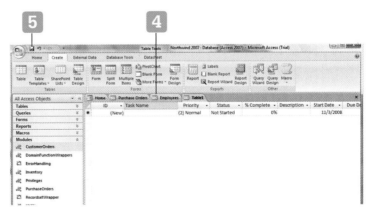

---

**? DID YOU KNOW?**

A field in a table can have more than one value. For example, you can assign a task to more than one person.

# Enter and find new table records

Once you have created a table, you need to work with the fields within it. A 'field' contains a type of information – an order date, product name, quantity. You enter the data into one field at a time. A toolbar just above the status bar at the bottom of the table helps you to create new records or move from one to another as you work.

**1** In the Navigation pane, click the Tables object and double-click the table that you want to open.

**2** Click the New Record button.

**3** Press Tab to accept the AutoNumber entry.

**4** Type the data.

**5** Press Tab to move to the next field.

**6** Click one of the Record buttons. Options are:

- First Record
- Previous Record
- Specific Record
- Next Record
- Last Record.

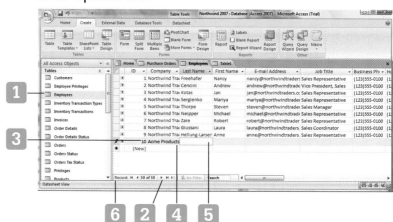

**? DID YOU KNOW?**

Click the Table Design button on the Create tab to add or delete rows or columns or change other aspects of the table's design.

**! ALERT:** The first field in a table is usually one called AutoNumber, which assigns a unique number to each record. You cannot select or change this field's value.

# Find records

Tables can contain thousands of fields and finding specific information can be difficult. The quickest option is to use Access's built-in search function.

**1** Double-click the table you want to open.

**2** Click Find button on the Home tab in the Find group.

**3** In the Find and Replace dialogue box that opens, type the text you want to find.

**4** Click the down arrow for the Look In box to select a search location.

**5** Click the Match dropdown list to select the type of match you want.

**6** Click Find Next.

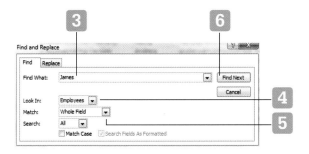

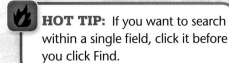

**? DID YOU KNOW?**
You can narrow your search further by choosing the Match Case option to match upper or lower case.

**🔥 HOT TIP:** If you want to search within a single field, click it before you click Find.

# Create a database query

A 'query' is a question that you submit to a database in order to extract the information you need. Queries are far more complex and powerful than the Find utility as they allow you to compile complex sets of data. The Query Wizard is a good place to get started with creating such queries.

**1** Click the Create tab.

**2** Click the Query Wizard button in the Other group.

**3** Click Simple Query Wizard, then click OK.

**4** Select a table for your query or select a query from the list.

**5** Click fields you want included in the query and click the right arrow to move the fields to the right side of the dialogue box.

**6** When you've finished, click Next.

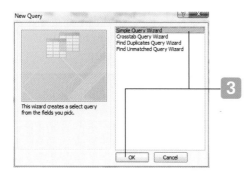

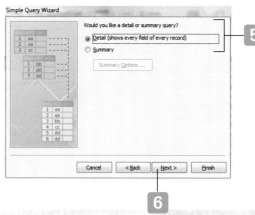

**? DID YOU KNOW?**

If you choose a numeric or date field for the query, be sure to indicate whether you want to see detailed or summary information. If you choose to see a summary, click Summary Options and then click OK.

**? DID YOU KNOW?**

Results of a query are listed under the Queries bar in the Navigation pane.

# Configure and view query results

Once you have composed a query (as shown in the preceding task), you choose from the options to specify how the results will be presented.

**1** Choose to see Detail or Summary results.

**2** Click Next.

**3** Enter a name for your query in the What title do you want for your query? box.

**4** Click Finish.

**5** View the results in the Reading pane.

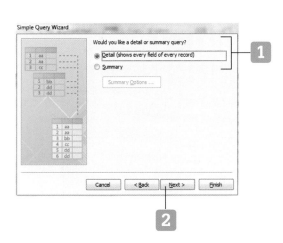

# Create a form, Part 1

In order to create a database, you need to enter the data. Clicking from one field to another and typing data can be time-consuming, particularly if the fields are far apart in the file – in different tables, for instance.

A form gives you a user-friendly way to carry out data entry. It can enter data in multiple tables, for instance. The quickest way to create a form is to use Access' built-in Form Wizard.

**1** Click the Create tab.

**2** Click the More Forms button in the Forms group and choose Form Wizard from the list that pops up.

**3** Choose a table or query on which to base your form.

**4** Click the fields you want and move them to the right-hand side of the dialogue box.

**5** Click Next.

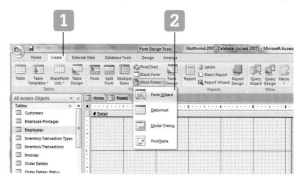

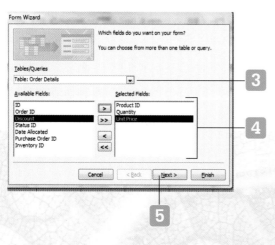

**? DID YOU KNOW?**

Other buttons available on the Create tab in the Forms group let you create a blank, basic or split form, among others.

# Create a form, Part 2

After you have started defining the fields for your form, you need to choose its design style and assign a name to it.

1. Choose the type of form layout you want.

2. Click Next.

3. Choose a style for the form.

4. Click Next.

5. Enter a name for the form in the What title do you want for your form? box.

6. Click Finish.

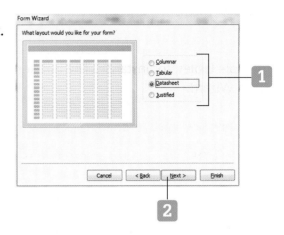

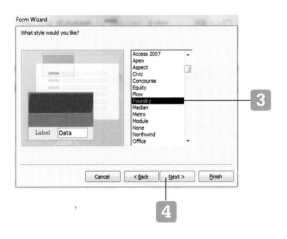

 **DID YOU KNOW?**

The style of the form is important because it affects its formatting and final appearance. Look closely at the preview that appears on the left side of the dialogue box to check that it's what you want.

# Enter data into a form

Once you have created a form, you can enter data into it.

**1** Click the Forms button in the Navigation pane.

**2** Double-click the form you want from the list to open it.

**3** Type data into the first field.

**4** Press Tab to move to the next field and enter data into it.

**5** When you have finished, click New Record to enter another record.

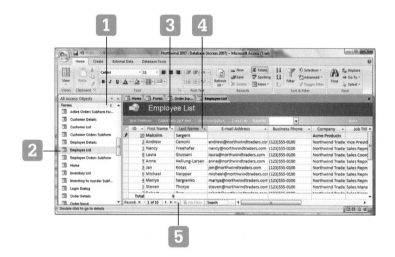

 **HOT TIP:** Press Shift + Tab to move to the previous field if you need to edit data that you have already entered.

# Create a report

To produce a report with Access, you can use one of the buttons in the Reports group on the Create tab. They let you create a basic report or blank report. You can also use the Report Wizard, which is a user-friendly way to select the information you want to present.

**1** Click the Reports button on the Navigation pane.

**2** Click the table you want to use in the report.

**3** Click Create.

**4** Click the Report Wizard button in the Reports group.

**5** Choose the table or query on which you want to base the form from the Tables/Queries box.

**6** Choose the fields you want to include and move them to the right-hand side of the dialogue box.

**7** Click Next. In the subsequent screens, you have the opportunity to specify any groupings of records and the order of records within each group. You can also choose the layout of the report and its style.

**8** Name your report, then click Finish.

**? DID YOU KNOW?**

If you have a table open and active and you click a report button, Access creates a report based on that table.

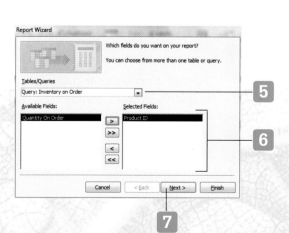

# Change page setup

Once you have created a report or form, it's a good idea to pay attention to the page setup, which means the margins, paper size, orientation and any grid and column settings.

**1** In the Navigation pane, click the report, form, table or other object for which you want to change the setup.

**2** Click the Office button, point to Print, then click the Print Preview tab.

**3** Click the Margins button and choose from Normal, Wide or Narrow.

**4** Click Size and select the size you want: Letter, Legal, A5 and so on.

**5** Click Portrait or Landscape orientation.

**6** Click Close Print Preview.

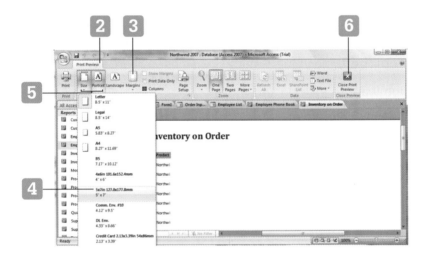

**? DID YOU KNOW?**

'Portrait' orientates the page so that its length is greater than its width, while landscape orientates it so that its width is greater than its length.

# Back up a database

It's always important to back up your electronic data. Backups are especially important when you have spent considerable time compiling and formatting databases and those databases are full of critical personal or business information. Access streamlines the process of backing up databases, requiring just a single command.

1 Save and close all your database objects.

2 Click the Office button.

3 Point to Manage and choose Back Up Database from the list.

4 Click Save As and select a location for the backup.

5 Change the backup name to something different from the original file name.

6 Click Save.

---

**! ALERT:** Don't save your backup on the same computer or disk as the original. Save it on a removable disk or network drive so that you have one or more copies in more than one location.

**? DID YOU KNOW?**

You can compact a database, including a backup, so that it takes up less disk space. Open the file, click Office, point to Manage, then click the Compact and Repair Database option on the list.

# 9 Getting organised with Outlook

# Introduction

The programs described in preceding chapters give you sophisticated ways to manage information. An essential aspect of working with such information is communication. In order to collaborate with friends and business colleagues, you need to be able to contact them and communicate the information you have gathered. Outlook 2007 gives you a user-friendly yet powerful way to both organise events and contacts and reach people.

Outlook helps you to keep track of appointments and meetings with its calendar. It also makes it easy to store contact information, from addresses and phone numbers for all your friends and family members to those of business associates. Its Notes feature allows you to write reminders to yourself and its Tasks feature gives you a place to assemble a 'to do' list. It's a fully featured email application as well.

This chapter's tasks will help you to organise your day-to-day activities with features that are easy to use and easy to customise as well. You'll be up and running in no time and the functions will let you meet all of your digital communications needs.

# Start Outlook for the first time

The first time you start Outlook, you are given the opportunity to configure your personal profile. Don't skip these steps: they guide you through the information that you need to send and receive email and set up contacts in address books.

**1** Start Outlook by clicking the Start button, pointing to All Programs, clicking Microsoft Office, and choosing Microsoft Office Outlook 2007.

**2** When the Welcome screen appears, click Next.

**3** In the next screen, when you are asked to configure an email account, click Yes.

**4** Click Next.

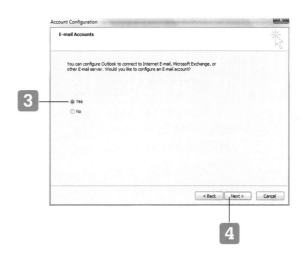

---

**?** **DID YOU KNOW?**

If you don't have your email account information ready, click No. You can add your account information later on.

**?** **DID YOU KNOW?**

You can configure Outlook to work with another email account at any time. Click Tools, click Account Settings, click the E-mail tab, click Add, then follow the instructions given by the Wizard that appears to help you set up the account.

5 Type your email account information into the boxes for Auto Account Setup.

6 Click Next. A dialogue box appears, showing the progress of the process of connecting to your email server.

7 When the connection has been established, click Finish.

8 When a dialogue box appears asking if you want to establish an RSS (Real Simple Syndication) feed, click Yes if you want to receive such feeds.

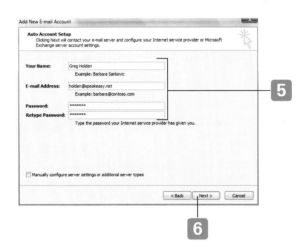

5

6

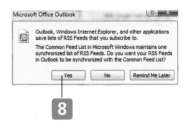

8

**? DID YOU KNOW?**

A 'profile' is a set of information needed to access one or more address books or email accounts.

**! ALERT:** In order to make full use of Outlook's email, scheduling and contact capabilities, you need to be connected to the Internet or a local area network (LAN). A high-speed service, such as a digital subscriber line (DSL) or cable connection, is optimal.

# Customise your 'to do' list

One of the best ways to get started with Outlook is to preview your meetings, appointments and tasks for the day using a feature called Outlook Today. It gives you a convenient place to see all of the day's events.

**1** Click the Outlook Today button on the left side of the Advanced toolbar. The Outlook Today page opens in the Outlook reading pane.

**2** Click Customize Outlook Today at the top right of that pane to change the feature's settings.

**3** Change the options you want.

**4** Click Save Changes.

Standard toolbar

Advanced toolbar

Reading pane

**ALERT:** In order to get a list of the day's events, you need to have entered them beforehand. Get in the habit of doing this so that you can track them as needed.

**DID YOU KNOW?**
If you don't see the Advanced toolbar, click View, point to Toolbars and choose Advanced from the dropdown menu.

# Add a task

In order to view tasks on your Outlook Today page, you need to have entered them beforehand. It only takes a few seconds to do so and you can add tasks for any date you wish.

**1** Click the Tasks view bar in the Navigation pane.

**2** Click the box that is initially labelled Type a new task and enter your own text. In the image below, I have typed 'Pick up prescription'.

**3** Press Enter.

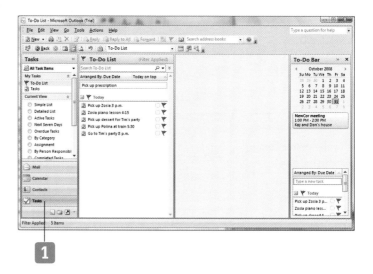

**HOT TIP:** To enter a task for a future date, select the data from the calendar at the top of the To-Do bar. Use the left and right arrows to move back or forwards one month, respectively.

# Enter a calendar item

A calendar item is different from a task. The Calendar can include appointments, meetings and other lists, not just tasks that you need to do. You can enter not only the date of the event but also the amount of time to allow for it in your schedule.

**1** Click the Calendar view bar.

**2** Choose a date.

**3** Scroll down to the desired time using the controls to the right of the Reading pane.

**4** Click the box next to the time you need, type the description, then press Enter.

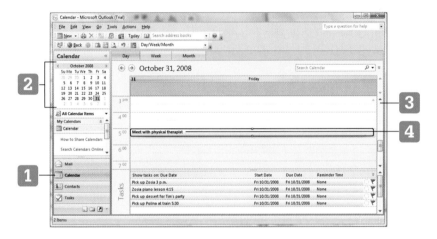

---

**? DID YOU KNOW?**

You can share your calendar with others on your network by clicking How to Share Calendars and following the instructions in the Help file that appears.

# Navigate through your Outlook data

The Navigation pane, which appears on the left side of the Outlook window, lets you move and enter data and view your information in different ways. By default, the Mail, Calendar, Contacts and Tasks view bars appear near the bottom of the pane. You can add more views by clicking the Configure button's dropdown arrow.

**1** Click a calendar date to view or enter tasks and other information for that date.

**2** Click one of the View buttons at the bottom of the Navigation pane to view a particular type of data.

**3** Click the Close button to close the Navigation pane.

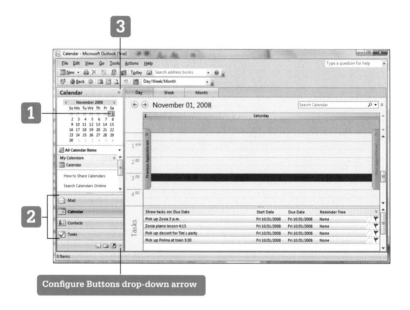

Configure Buttons drop-down arrow

**? DID YOU KNOW?**

The Go menu gives you an alternative way to navigate through Outlook. It's a good option if you have closed the Navigation pane.

**? DID YOU KNOW?**

The double arrows in the upper right-hand corner of the Navigation pane let you minimise or maximise it. Click to minimise the pane when you need more room to work with information in the Reading pane.

# Customise the Navigation pane

You might not know the full range of information that the Outlook pane can provide unless you customise it. You can add or remove the view buttons at the bottom of the pane or change their order.

**1** Click the Configure Buttons dropdown arrow, point to Add or Remove Buttons, then choose a button from the menu.

**2** To change the order of the buttons or add or remove buttons, click Configure Buttons and choose Navigation Pane Options.

**3** To display a button, make sure that the box next to it has been ticked.

**4** To remove a button, untick the box next to it.

**5** To reorder the buttons, click one you want to move, then click Move Up or Move Down.

**6** When you're happy, click OK.

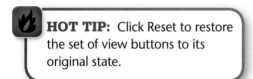

**HOT TIP:** Click Reset to restore the set of view buttons to its original state.

# View items

Each of the views listed in the Navigation pane (Mail, Calendar, Contacts, Tasks and so on) has folders within it. Within each of those folders, the individual items that make up your Outlook data are stored. You can then edit, delete or organise each item as needed.

**1** Click one of the View buttons in the Navigation pane to switch to the Outlook view you want. In the images below, Tasks view is chosen.

**2** Click the Current View down arrow.

**3** Choose a view that you want to use.

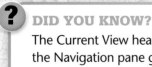

---

**?** **DID YOU KNOW?**

The Current View heading in the Navigation pane gives you a second place to work with different subsections within an overall view.

# View folders

Each of your tasks, contacts or other bits of information is stored within a folder. You can view and edit the folders as you wish by choosing them in the Navigation pane.

**1** Click the Folder List icon at the bottom of the Navigation pane.

**2** Click a folder in the list to view its contents in the Reading pane.

**3** Right-click an item and choose New Folder from the context menu to create a new subfolder within the main folder.

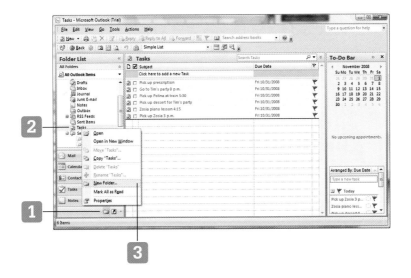

**HOT TIP:** The Search Folders item at the bottom of the list of folders lets you search your email for different criteria. A search folder is a virtual folder with criteria you might want to search (all email with attachments, for instance). By default, you have three search folders: Categorized Mail, Large Mail and Unread Mail. You can create a new search folder by clicking Mail view, clicking the File menu, pointing to New and clicking search folder. In the New search folder dialogue box, click any one of the predefined search folders and then customise it so it has the criteria you want.

# Subscribe to an RSS feed

Outlook includes a reader for Really Simple Syndication (RSS) feeds that keep you up to date with blogs, news feeds or other information on the Web.

In order to receive a feed, put out by a blog or website, you need to subscribe to it. You can do so within either Internet Explorer or Outlook. This task shows you how to subscribe using Outlook.

**1** Right-click the RSS feed displayed on a Web page and click Copy Link Location on the context menu that appears.

**2** Switch to Outlook and click Folder List if necessary.

**3** Right-click the RSS Feeds folder and choose Add a New RSS Feed from the context menu.

**HOT TIP:** Click the plus sign next to the RSS Feeds folder. You'll find that you are already subscribed to several feeds.

**DID YOU KNOW?**

If you browse to a website that provides an RSS feed, you can click the RSS Feeds link and then click Subscribe to this feed. You can then read the feed using Outlook.

# Add a new contact

Contacts are fundamental pieces of information that you can track and work with in Outlook. A 'contact' is a person or business you need to communicate with, by phone, fax, IM, text or email. Outlook can help you with all of these media: it gives you a way to store names, addresses and contact information, as well as other essential information about each contact, such as birthdays, account information, company names or titles.

1 Click the Contacts view button in the Navigation pane.

2 Click New in the toolbar.

3 When the Contact window opens, fill in the contact information. The Contact window contains its own set of Ribbon tabs: Contact, Insert, Format Text and Developer.

4 When you enter a phone number, fill in your current location in the Location Information dialogue box and then click OK.

5 Click Details on the Contacts tab in the Show group and fill in more detailed information about the contact.

6 Click the Save & Close button to the left of the Contacts tab in the Actions group.

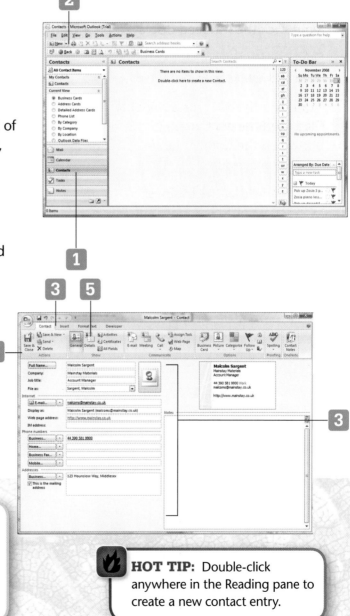

 **DID YOU KNOW?**

In the process of creating a contact, you also create an electronic business card, which you can share with others as an email attachment.

**HOT TIP:** Double-click anywhere in the Reading pane to create a new contact entry.

# Display and edit a business card

An electronic business card (EBC) is the 'short version' of a contact. It is created in the process of assembling contact information. The EBC appears in the upper right-hand corner of the Contacts window. It includes the person's name, company name, job title, phone number and other basic contact details.

1 Click the Contacts view button in the Navigation pane.

2 Double-click the contact you want to view in the Contacts window.

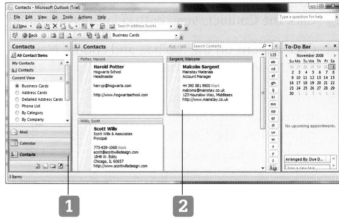

3 Click the Business Card button on the Contact tab in the Options group.

4 Click the field of the business card you want to edit from the list.

5 Make the changes you want.

6 Click OK.

**HOT TIP:** Click Reset Card to remove any formatting changes you made if you want to be left with a generic card.

# Create a distribution list

A 'distribution list' is a set of contacts that you can treat as a single entity. It's similar to a 'mailing list' in the world of email – that is, you can send a single message or task request to a designated group as a whole. Thus, instead of having to communicate with each list member individually, you can send a message to everyone on your list at once.

**1** Click the Contacts view button in the Navigation pane.

**2** Click Actions on the toolbar, and choose New Distribution List from the list that pops up. The Distribution List window opens.

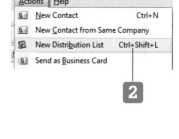

**3** Type a name for your distribution list in the Name box.

**4** Click the Select Members button in the Members group.

**5** Select the names that you want to add to your new distribution list.

**6** Click the Members button in the Show group. You will see your new list.

**7** Click OK.

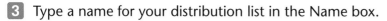
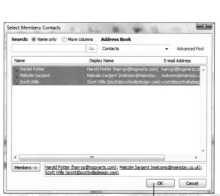

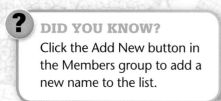
**HOT TIP:** Press Ctrl + Shift + L to quickly open the Distribution List window.

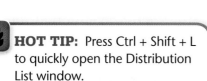
**? DID YOU KNOW?**
Click the Add New button in the Members group to add a new name to the list.

# Create and address an email message

One of Outlook's most basic functions is the sending and receiving of email messages. You do so in the Untitled Message window. You address the message, type the text, check over what you've typed, then click Send.

**1** Click the Mail button in the Navigation pane.

**2** Click the New button.

**3** Enter the email address of the recipient, or click the To button and choose a recipient from your list of contacts.

**4** Click Cc, if necessary, to choose any recipients who should also receive the message.

**5** Enter the subject of your message in the next box.

**6** Type your message.

**7** Click Spelling in the Proofing group to check the spelling of your message.

**8** Click Send.

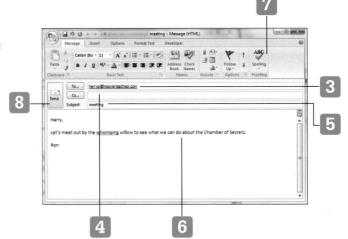

 **HOT TIP:** You can send a message to multiple addresses by separating each recipient in the To box with a semicolon (;). Press Enter after each email address and the semicolon will be entered automatically.

# Attach a file to an email message

An attachment is an image, text or other file you send along with the text of an email message. Because you're using Outlook 2007, you have the added advantage of being able to send an Outlook task, contact or note.

1 Once you have composed your email message text, click the Attach Item or Attach File icon in the Include group on the Message tab, which appears at the top of the Message window.

2 In the Insert File dialogue box that appears, locate the file you want to attach.

3 Click Insert. The filename will appear in the Attached box at the top of your message.

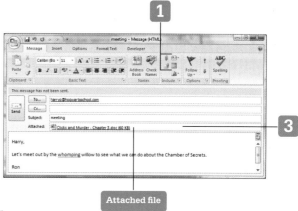

Attached file

**ALERT:** Take care to monitor the size of your attachments. Files over 1MB in size (such as digital photos) not only take a long time to send, but they may be blocked by some email services. To send a large attachment, pack it in a file archive program, such as WinZip (http://www.winzip.com).

# Create a signature file

A 'signature file' is a bit of text that you can add to the end of all your email messages. Signature files can identify you and even help you to market yourself and your business. You don't have to type a signature file every time you end a message; by saving the information you need in a text file, you can have Outlook add it automatically.

**1** Click the Tools menu, click Options.

**2** When the Options dialogue box opens, click the Mail Format tab.

**3** Click Signatures.

**4** Click New, type a name for your signature file, then click OK.

**5** Type your signature file text.

**6** Click OK twice.

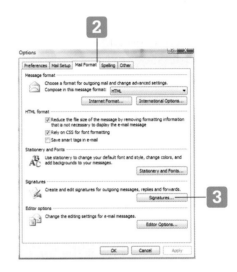

---

**? DID YOU KNOW?**

Use the formatting controls in the Signatures and Stationery dialogue box to give your signature file some graphic interest. Select the text you want to format and click the controls to make it bold, centred or add a hyperlink.

**? DID YOU KNOW?**

Be sure to type a short and easy-to-remember name for your signature file so that you can find it easily. You can have more than one signature file, for different purposes.

# Send an email message

When you have the text of your email message and attached files and signatures as needed, you can send it. You can send and receive messages at the same time, as well as control the way Outlook sends messages. When you send a message, Outlook moves it to the Outbox folder, where it stays while Outlook connects to your email server and sends the mail.

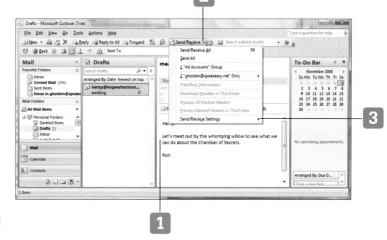

**1** Create your message.

**2** Click the Send button to simply send the message, or click the Send/Receive down arrow in the toolbar to choose a send option:

- Send All sends all messages that you have ready to send in all of your email accounts

- Send <account name> sends only messages that are ready in the specified email account.

**3** Choose Send/Receive Settings at the bottom of the list, then choose Send/Receive Groups to change the way Outlook sends and receives emails.

**4** Click the New, Edit, Copy, Remove or Rename buttons to change the settings for your selected account group or all accounts.

**5** Click or untick the tick boxes for the send and receive options you want in the bottom half of the box.

**6** Click Close, then click OK.

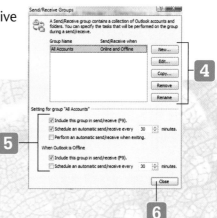

**? DID YOU KNOW?**

To insert a miniature version of your calendar in an email message, click the Insert tab at the top of the message window, then click the Calendar button.

# Reading email messages

You don't necessarily have to do anything to have Outlook retrieve your email. As long as your computer is connected to the Internet and Outlook is open, the program will check for and receive your email at regular intervals. You can also click Send/Receive to have Outlook check your mail and retrieve any incoming messages at any other time.

**1** To check for incoming messages, click the Send/Receive button on the toolbar. If a message arrives, you will see an alert in the taskbar. An envelope icon appears to let you know that a message is ready for you to read.

**2** Click the message header in the Inbox navigation pane to display the message.

**3** Read the message in the Message pane.

**4** To open an attachment, double-click the file to open it or:

- Right-click the attachment, click Save As, find a location, then click OK

- Click the attachment, then click Preview File.

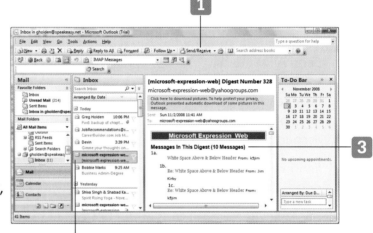

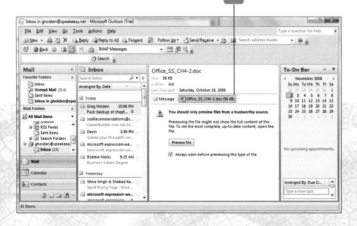

# Searching your email

If you have let your email pile up to hundreds or even thousands of messages, it can be a challenge to find a message from a particular individual or with a particular keyword in the subject line. Outlook, however, makes it easy for you to search for and locate the messages you want.

**1** Click the Mail view button.

**2** Click the Query Builder button in the Instant Search bar to open the Instant Search pane.

**3** Enter your criteria in the From, To and other boxes in the Query Builder boxes. The search results automatically appear beneath the Instant Search pane.

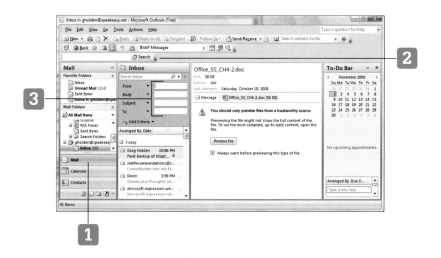

# Top 10 Office 2007 Problems solved

# Introduction

One of Office 2007's most useful features is its ability to diagnose and repair problems that you might encounter. In the course of working with Word, Excel or another application, you might detect that the program is working slower than it did earlier. The cause might be that, in the course of moving files, you have separated data needed by Access or Excel, for example, so it takes longer to locate. More serious problems – such as corrupted software due to viruses – can also be detected.

Each application has its own repair options and Office itself has a diagnostic utility that works with each of its components. In the event that you can't resolve a problem using the Office Diagnostics utility, you can reinstall Office. You're not on your own even with this task as you can use Office Setup's maintenance feature to remove features or reinstall Office if the need arises.

# Problem 1: An Office program doesn't seem to be running properly

The first line of defence, if you find that an Office application isn't operating properly, is to use the Office Diagnostics application. This feature is available to all of Office's applications. Use it if you see an alert message or other indications that your Office program can't find data, is running slowly or is experiencing mixups with data stored in the Windows registry.

**1** Click the Office button.

**2** Click <Program> Options.

**3** Click Resources.

**4** Click Diagnose.

**5** When a Microsoft Office Diagnostics dialogue box appears, click Continue.

**6** When a second Microsoft Office Diagnostics dialogue box appears, click Continue. The dialogue box notifies you of the progress of the check.

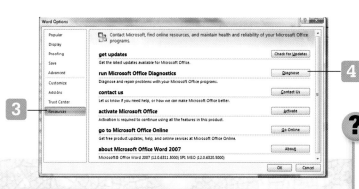

**HOT TIP:** In Outlook or Publisher, you need to click the Help menu and choose Office Diagnostics.

**? DID YOU KNOW?**

You can also access Office Diagnostics from Windows rather than from inside an application. Click Start, point to All Programs, click Microsoft Office, click Microsoft Office Tools, and then click Microsoft Office Diagnostics.

# Problem 2: How do I maintain or repair Office applications?

You don't need to perform diagnostic routines only when you encounter problems with the way applications are operating. You can also perform routine maintenance to make sure that your programs are running smoothly. This might be particularly useful if you are preparing a critical project that involves one or more Office programs.

**1** Insert your Office 2007 CD.

**2** In Windows Explorer or My Computer, double-click the Setup icon.

**3** Click one or more of the maintenance buttons:

- Add or Remove Features lets you change features that you have installed

- Repair lets you reinstall or repair Office 2007

- Remove lets you remove Office 2007 altogether.

**4** Click Continue and follow instructions on the Wizard that appears.

**5** If you clicked Add or Remove Features, you have the chance to choose applications or components within them that you want to add or remove.

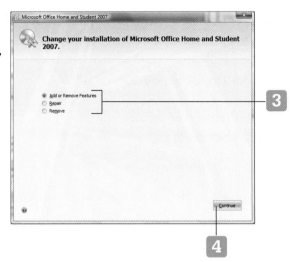

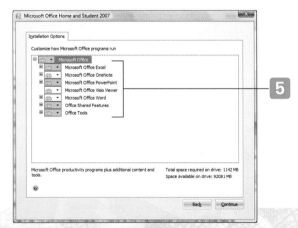

**? DID YOU KNOW?**

The Registry is a storehouse of critical information that your applications need to run. Often, when viruses attack your operating system, they plant false data in the Registry so applications can run that perform malicious functions, such as recording your keystrokes.

# Problem 3: I need to enable Safe mode, what do I do?

You might be familiar with Safe mode from problems with the Windows operating system. If the system encounters a serious problem, you have the option of starting in Safe mode to repair it. Office 2007 also switches to Safe mode when it encounters major difficulties.

In fact, Office uses two types of Safe mode: Automated and User-Initiated. If an Office program is not able to start up after encountering problems, it automatically starts in Safe mode the next time you try to use it. You may need to manually enable Safe mode yourself to make this option available.

1. Click the Office button and choose <Program> Options.

2. Click Trust Center in the left pane.

3. Click Trust Center Settings in the main pane.

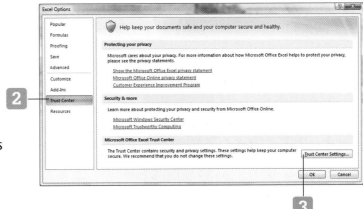

4. Click ActiveX Settings.

5. Click the tick box next to Safe mode (helps limit the control's access to your computer) in the main pane.

6. Click OK, then click OK in the next window to close it.

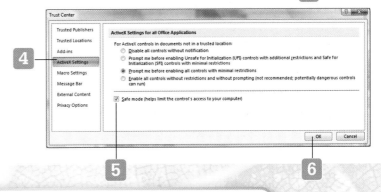

**ALERT:** When an Office program starts in Safe mode, some of its features are unavailable – you can't save templates, for instance. Once you are in Safe mode, you can track which features are disabled in the Trust Center. You can enable them one at a time to pinpoint the problem.

# Problem 4: How do I start user-initiated Safe mode?

If you encounter problems with one or more Office applications and it or they do not go into Safe mode automatically, you can start it up yourself with user-initiated Safe mode.

1 Click the Start button on the taskbar.

2 Click All Programs.

3 Double-click Microsoft Office.

4 Press and hold down the Ctrl key.

5 Choose the program you want to open from the list.

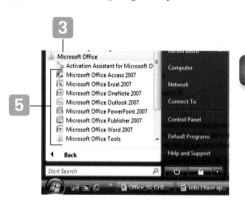

**HOT TIP:** You can also use the Run menu to start a program in user-initiated Safe mode. Click the Start button, then type Run in the box at the bottom of the Start menu. Select Run, press Enter, then start the program by adding the safe instruction at the end of the command line.

# Problem 5: I need to correct an Excel formula

Formulas in Excel can quickly become complicated, but tools are available to help you track down problems.

One, the Watch Window, keeps track of cells that you specify. If you make changes to a worksheet that affect the cells and any formulas associated with them, the Watch Window lets you know about problems.

**1** Open the worksheet that you want to monitor, then select the cells you want to watch.

**2** Click the Formulas tab.

**3** Click Watch Window, in the Formula Auditing group.

**4** Click the Add Watch button on the Watch Window task bar.

**5** Click Add.

**6** Click Close.

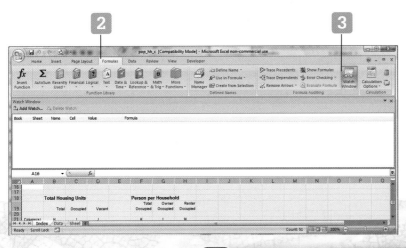

**HOT TIP:** To select all of a worksheet's cells at once, click the button in the upper-left corner, which simply has an arrow pointing down and to the right. Otherwise, click and drag over the cells to select them.

# Problem 6: I need to check an Excel worksheet for errors

The Error Checker is another automated feature that tracks any errors in your worksheet formulas. It follows rules that apply to formula preparation to uncover problems. The Error Checker works in the background, so you can carry on editing your worksheet.

**1** Open the worksheet you want to check for errors.

**2** Click the Formulas tab.

**3** Click the Error Checking button in the Formula Auditing group, then choose Error Checking from the dropdown list. The Error Checker automatically scans the worksheet for errors.

**4** Click Resume if needed.

**5** If an error is found a box reporting what it is will pop up. Choose one of the buttons to handle the problem. For instance, click Trace Empty Cell to point to the cell that contains the problem.

**6** Click Previous or Next to proceed with the check. When you've finished, click Close.

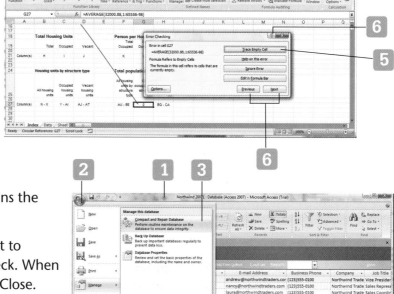

**?** **DID YOU KNOW?**

You can specify error-checking options before you use the Error Checker. Click Office, click Excel Options, click Formulas, then tick the Enable background error checking box. Select the error checking rule tick boxes you want, then click OK.

# Problem 7: I think my Access database needs repairing

If you encounter problems with an Access 2007 database – for instance, if the program crashes when you try to gather data – it might mean the database has become corrupted or too large. Access has a utility that can repair many of the problems that can cause databases to be corrupted.

1 Open the database you want to repair.

2 Click the Office button.

3 Point to Manage and choose Compact and Repair Database.

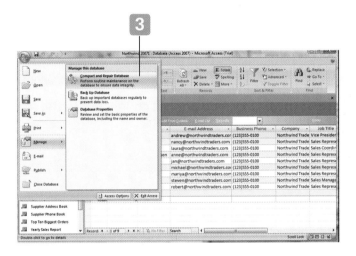

 **SEE ALSO:** See Chapter 8 for more on maintaining databases, including compacting them to keep them to a manageable size.

# Problem 8: I can't send or receive emails

It's not unusual to press Outlook's Send and Receive button only to discover that the program cannot perform this function. Usually, it means that Outlook is unable to connect to your email server.

Before you call your Internet service provider's (ISP) support staff, you should try a few debugging procedures on your own. Often, you can troubleshoot the problem yourself.

1. If you are connected to the Internet via an ethernet cable, make sure the cable is plugged in securely to both your computer and your router.

2. Point to the network icon in the system tray. If you are attempting to retrieve emails from a remote server rather than your company or organisation's network, you should see the message Access: Local and Internet. If you see the message Access: Local Only, you are not connected to the Internet.

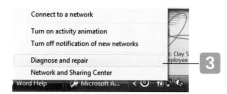

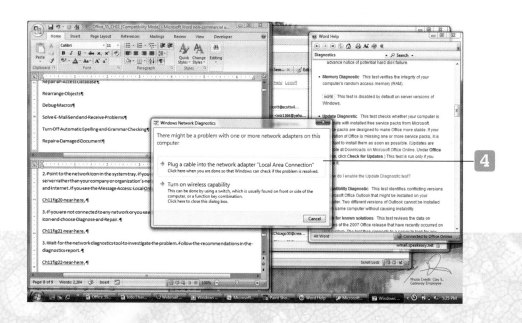

3. If you are not connected to any network or you see the Local Only message, right-click the Network icon and choose Diagnose and repair.

4. Wait for the Network Diagnostics tool to investigate the problem. Follow the recommendations in the diagnostics report.

5. If you have a wireless connection, right-click the network icon and choose Connect to a network.

6. Choose your preferred network from the list and click Connect.

7. If you cannot connect or if you connect but still don't have Internet access, restart your computer.

# Problem 9: How do I repair a damaged document?

Sometimes, you try to open a file and things go wrong. The file either doesn't open, opens slowly or doesn't open in its entirety. All Office programs have the ability to use a repair utility designed especially for damaged files.

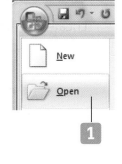

**1** Click the Office button and click Open to open the file that you need to repair.

**2** Click the Open down arrow.

**3** Choose Open and Repair to open and repair the damaged file.

**HOT TIP:** You can also open the file from the list of recent documents, if it appears there.

# Problem 10: I need to recover a damaged file

Microsoft Word has a special utility that can help you to recover text from a file that has been damaged. Use it if the option described in the preceding task fails to work.

1. Click the Office button and click Open.

2. Locate the file that you need to repair.

3. Click the All Files dropdown list.

4. Choose Recover Text from Any File from the list that appears.

5. When the Show Repairs dialogue box appears, click Close.

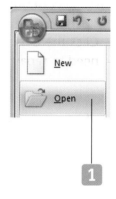